HIGH-CONFLICT
DIVORCE FOR WOMEN

HIGH- CONFLICT
DIVORCE
FOR
WOMEN

YOUR GUIDE TO COPING SKILLS
AND LEGAL STRATEGIES FOR
ALL STAGES OF DIVORCE

DEBRA DOAK

ROCKRIDGE
PRESS

Cover Designer: Liz Cosgrove
Interior Designer: Jen Cogliantry
Art Producer: Janice Ackerman
Editor: Barbara J. Isenberg
Production Editor: Mia Moran

Cover Stock Illustration: Peshkova/Shutterstock (torn paper); Alexander_IV/Shutterstock (background texture); Jiri Hera/Shutterstock (open book).

ISBN: Print 978-1-64152-819-1 | eBook 978-1-64152-820-7
R0

This book is dedicated to my
children, who continue to show
me what resilience looks like.
And to every strong woman who
has led the way for others.

CONTENTS

"Prepare the umbrella before it rains."

—MALAY PROVERB

INTRODUCTION

Divorce. For many, the process is amicable, tensions are temporary, and relationships can remain civil and intact. But for some, it feels more like a personal assault—even an all-out war—and if you aren't prepared, a sneak attack by the other side can leave you wounded.

Welcome to the world of high-conflict divorce.

You may have picked up this book because your spouse is an addict, an abuser, has anger issues, or suffers from mental illness. You know divorce is going to be difficult. Or maybe the love of your life morphed into someone you don't recognize, and you've been caught off guard by their vindictive and hostile behavior. Either way, I'm glad you're here, because high-conflict divorce has some characteristics that can make it stressful or even worse.

In my work as a CDC Certified Divorce Coach® and Certified Divorce Financial Analyst®, I see the fallout from high-conflict divorce, and as a survivor myself, I have the experience to empathize with what you're going through. I offer support, tools, information, and resources so my clients can enter the arena fully prepared and with their eyes wide open.

I have helped women work their way to the other side of a tumultuous divorce process with their grace and confidence intact. I've also seen some women make mistakes that cost them dearly. My goal is to inform and guide you toward actions that will help you maintain your well-being and achieve the most successful resolution possible.

The difference between standard divorce and high-conflict divorce is that in the latter, it seems that all bets are off and there are no rules for the opponent. While you follow the proper steps, tell the truth, and try to come to an equitable agreement, your partner's goal will be to win at all costs or to see you ruined. Just a few of the nasty tricks they may employ are:

- False allegations of abuse against them or your children
- Fraudulent use of your information to take out loans
- Cutting off financial support and hiding assets
- Cyber stalking or hacking
- Attempts to alienate your children
- Delays, obstruction, or downright refusal to comply with court orders
- Verbal, physical, or social media harassment

The earlier you can detect high-conflict divorce might be in your future, the better prepared you can be to protect yourself and build up your support system.

WHAT TO LOOK FOR

So, how do you know if you are headed for a standard, slightly contentious divorce or if you are about to walk into the battle zone of high-conflict divorce? Past behavior is the best indicator of future behavior, so if your spouse has been toxic throughout your marriage, you can be pretty certain they will ramp up the crazy during divorce.

Unfortunately, divorce can bring out the beast in your previously go-along, get-along, relatively lovely spouse, too. Here are a few signs to look for:

Threats and declaration of outcomes:
"You'll never see your kids again."
"You'll never get a penny of spousal support."
"You'll be on the streets."
"You'll be sorry."
"I'm going to bury you."

Withdrawal of financial support:
Secrecy, large withdrawals, sale of assets, or redirection of their paycheck into a new account

Refusal to communicate:
Failure to reply to texts, e-mails, or calls regarding settlement issues or the children; claims that they never received your messages

Harassment:
Stalking, spying, hacking your phone, computer, or e-mail, or posting nasty messages on social media
Badmouthing you
Telling untrue stories about you to family, friends, or church

If you recognize any of these or other radical changes in behavior, then this book is for you. I'll give you strategies to persevere, protect yourself, avoid common mistakes, and save some of your sanity along the way.

HOW TO USE THIS BOOK

High-conflict people don't limit their destructive behavior to one part of the process, so this book is divided into three sections:

Part One: Before a High-Conflict Divorce
Part Two: During Divorce Proceedings
Part Three: After the Divorce

Each section offers specific strategies for addressing the psychological, legal, and custody issues you are likely to face during that particular stage.

Feel free to skip to the section or topic that you need immediate help with. There's no need to read this book front-to-back to get advice for the situation you're facing. Take what you need right now.

It takes a team to navigate high-conflict divorce. This book will give you lots of practical help, but it should not be used in a vacuum. You will still need an experienced attorney, a savvy financial advisor, a coach or therapist, and others to guide you safely through the process.

Speaking of safety, it is widely known that abuse can escalate when a victimized spouse makes the decision to separate. The perpetrator can become enraged and may go to any length, including physical violence, to try to regain power. Be on the lookout for early warning signs so you can put proactive safety measures in place.

If you have concerns that you or your children are in danger, please call the National Domestic Violence Hotline at 1-800-799-SAFE (7233) at any time, night or day, to speak with an advocate about a safety plan.

Finally, at the end of the book, you will find a list of recommended resources for additional help with managing emotions, communication, co-parenting, finances, recovery, and more.

Although high-conflict divorce is filled with uncertainties, there is so much you can do to help yourself prepare. And the sooner and more fully you prepare, the better off you will be in every way.

PART
ONE

BEFORE A HIGH-CONFLICT DIVORCE

Whether you're just beginning to think about divorce, or your divorce is already in motion, you are wise to start preparing for what's ahead. The next few chapters will assist you in taking steps to equip yourself for what you might face in a high-conflict divorce.

First, we'll walk through the process of getting yourself emotionally ready to tackle the overwhelming confusion and stress that can result from high-conflict divorce. Later we will explore ways to mitigate that stress through lifestyle adjustments, but first I'll offer strategies for protecting yourself and getting the right support, and talking to friends and family about your divorce.

In chapter 2, I'll introduce some of the legal and financial concepts you'll encounter, give you tips for finding the right attorney, and show you how to gather the documentation you'll need.

Finally, if you have children, you may be more concerned with their feelings than your own. Chapter 3 offers guidance about how to talk to your children about divorce, understand and help them process their reactions, and answer common questions.

CHAPTER ONE

PREPARING YOURSELF EMOTIONALLY

Preparation and the right support are keys to surviving high-conflict divorce with grace. Your spouse may be doing everything in their power to hurt you or try to get you to lash out, back down, or make a wrong move. It's easy to get caught up in the drama. But when you know what to expect, you can step back, remain calm, and stay focused on what's in your best interest.

Some women are already braced for a high-conflict divorce. Their spouses were abusers or addicts, suffered from mental illness, or were just generally toxic people. These women know they are in for a battle. You may be one of these women. Despite this knowledge, even a spouse who was very difficult during the marriage can surprise you by taking it up a few notches during divorce.

Ashley, a client of mine, knew what she was in for:

> *"I knew it would be hateful; he has always loved 'the fight.' In fact, when I first broached the conversation with him to tell him I wasn't happy in our marriage, his immediate response was, 'If you ever leave me, things will get real ugly, real fast.'"*

Conversely, perhaps you've been blindsided. It's like a switch got flipped and your previously sweet, reasonable partner is now hateful. Attempts to communicate with them are returned with silence, demands, or threats.

This personality change can be hard to come to terms with and might leave you wondering:

> *Is this something that has been lurking all along?*
> *What caused this behavior to show up now?*
> *Is someone egging them on?*
> *Do they have a brain tumor or dementia?*
> *Have they had a psychotic break?*

What in the world is going on?

My client Tam explains it this way:

*"This person I loved and lived with for almost 50 years looked at
me one day with contempt and hatred in his eyes, said, 'Get out,'
and then went on to say other really awful things. This was not
the man that I had dinner with the night before. His behavior
over the next few weeks was so bizarre, so threatening, so fright-
ening, I was worried he had a brain tumor or a stroke. I was
really torn between caring about him and needing to protect
myself."*

Because you may still care about them, it's common to
wonder if there is a medical or physical reason for a radical
change in behavior. Regardless of the cause, it's still important
to be in self-protection mode. Your best course of action is to
share that concern with a friend or family member of theirs
and then take that off your plate. They are in good hands, and
you can return your attention to taking care of yourself.

A Necessary Shift in Thinking

Warm, fuzzy memories of your married past can prevent you
from taking the steps you need to take going forward. The
person you married is not the person you are divorcing, and
failure to remember that can cost you.

High-conflict divorce is a tricky new world where you
must look out for yourself. You can start by being mindful
of what you say and how you say it. For example, you may
be tempted to lash out at your soon-to-be ex by sending
angry texts or e-mails, or saying things to your children
about the other parent, but this kind of behavior has many

negative repercussions. We'll explore these more later, but it's important to know that displays of anger can result in unfavorable settlement rulings or even negative custody outcomes. It is well worth the effort—a golden rule of sorts—to remain calm in front of partners and children, and save the venting for a trusted friend, family member, divorce coach, or therapist.

We'll talk more in chapter 4 about the emotions you'll be feeling and how to manage them, but for now, I want to give you some tools to ensure that you don't let your own anger hurt you.

Changing How You Communicate

Emotions are high, everyone's mad, and a lot is at stake. And if you're trying to communicate with a high-conflict person, it's going to require a new set of skills and a renewed sense of strength and resolve not to let yourself be shaken by the blaming, shaming, and lies that you may now be hearing. Here are a few tools to help you:

Communicate only in writing. One of the smartest precautions you can take is to do all your communication in writing. You will be less likely to say something you regret, and you will have a record of all your conversations, including everything your partner has said to you.

Keep it brief and straightforward. Your words can be used against you, so respond as if your words will be read in court. The best way to do this is to keep all necessary communication short, polite, and straightforward. Avoid any tempting jabs or commentary.

An effective tool for dealing with high-conflict people is known as the BIFF Response Method, which states that all correspondence should be:

- Brief
- Informative
- Friendly
- Firm

See Resources (page 185) for more on the BIFF Response Method.

Avoid knee-jerk reactions. Before you reply to communication, ask yourself if you even need to respond. If you need to confirm a pick-up time, then yes. If you're being accused of lying and cheating, then no. You'll protect your own case, and you may even de-escalate the situation.

Check the Quick Guide in the back of the book (page 175) for some specific suggestions on responding to messages.

CREATING AN EMERGENCY PLAN

In high-conflict divorce, safety can become a priority. In some cases, a spouse isn't interested in just getting a more favorable settlement or a bit more time with the kids; rather, their objective is to win, even if it hurts you in the process.

Ashley said:

> *"I wanted to believe that as the father of my children, he wouldn't do anything to screw over me or our children. I couldn't have been more wrong. He didn't care who he hurt."*

A previously charming or timid spouse may use underhanded tricks to gain an advantage, and a partner with anger, control, or jealousy issues could go on full-out attack. Such attacks may be direct or physical in nature, such as stalking or abuse, while other attacks might involve attempts to sabotage your emotional or financial grounding.

Personally, I was blessed to have family members who gave me a place to live and helped support me when my spouse cut off financial support during our divorce. Many women aren't as lucky and need to get safety measures in place right away.

In any divorce, it's important to be vigilant and aware. But in high-conflict divorce, you must be prepared for an emergency at any time. Here are a few steps you can take now:

Safe People

Determine right away who you can count on to provide a safe space or support on short notice:

- Who can you call at 3:00 a.m. to come over or pick you up?
- Who can watch the kids for you or give them rides?
- Where could you and the kids stay for a few days or weeks?
- Who else might need to be aware of your circumstances (police, principal, guidance counselor, teacher, employer, family, neighbors, etc.)?
- Research local shelters and resources and have contact information readily available. Keep the National Domestic Violence Hotline number on hand: 1-800-799-SAFE (7233).

Safe Money

Don't fall victim to a tactic called "spousal starvation," in which your partner cuts off financial support or empties accounts to cripple you financially:

- Open a bank account in your name only (not where you did your joint banking).
- Get a credit card in your own name.
- Check your credit report.
- Begin accumulating money however you can: Stash your paycheck (or part of it), do odd jobs, sell items, get cash back on your debit card at the grocery store.

Safe Communication

Sneaky spouses may try to monitor you, your e-mail, calls, and texts, or install spyware on your phone or computer. Protect your privacy:

- Set up a new e-mail address with a password your spouse can't guess.
- Change passwords on all your personal accounts.
- Clear the cache, browser history, and cookies from your computer and phone.
- Set up new browser accounts if you share with your spouse.
- Establish your own cell phone plan (or get a prepaid phone) with a new number and share it only with trusted people.
- Forward your mail to a PO box or to a trusted friend's address.

Safe Storage

Documents, keepsakes, jewelry, and other items can go "missing" during high-conflict divorce. Your spouse may change passwords, preventing you from having access to the financial data you need:

- Rent a safe deposit box at your new bank, or make arrangements with a safe person to provide storage for you.
- Copy financial records such as tax returns, retirement statements, W-2s and so on. Store the copies in your safe location separate from the originals. See page 26 for a full list of documents you might need.
- Move passports, birth certificates, car titles, and jewelry to your safe place.

- Take photos or videos of items you aren't able to move, to document what was there.

My best advice to you is to prepare for the worst. It's better to have taken precautions you didn't need than to be caught with your guard down and suffer the consequences. We'll discuss building a support network of friends, family, and professionals to be part of your team later (page 15).

KEEPING TRACK

Your partner's goal may be to hurt you, damage your reputation, humiliate you, as well as:

- Turn others against you
- Remove you from your home
- Sabotage or destroy you financially
- Get custody of your children or threaten to do so
- Put you in jail
- Injure or hurt you

In any legal argument, documentation is boss. The side that presents the best case is typically the side that has the most credible and compelling evidence. In this section, we'll review the kind of records and documentation you'll want to gather. You may be in for a very big fight, so become a documentation fanatic.

Communication

Your first reaction might be to delete those aggressive text messages or e-mails, but don't do it. You may need them later. Screenshot, print, and save each harassing, disparaging, or threatening message or social media post as soon as it appears. In this day of electronic communication, what was there yesterday may not be there tomorrow. Posts can be removed, and your phone or e-mail account could be closed or hacked, preventing you from accessing this information later.

The same rule applies for any evidence you are gathering for your case, such as social media posts of your spouse with their affair partner on vacation, showing off the boat they bought, partying, or behaving badly. Any messages you have that support your case should also be printed, copied, and stored in your safe location.

Threats, Harassment, or Violence

Not every high-conflict divorce reaches a dangerous level, but if yours does, you must be prepared to stay safe and document what happened. Here are suggestions:

Report to local law enforcement. If your partner hurts, threatens, or stalks you, destroys property, or enters your residence without permission, call your local law enforcement agency to make a report. These reports will become an important part of your case and may support your requests for a protection order, exclusive use of your marital residence, custody, or visitation.

Take photos or videos. Photos and/or videos of marital property can be important to prove 1) items existed in case they go missing, and 2) their original and altered condition if they get damaged. Photos and videos can also help your attorney or a judge understand the extent of any damages, injuries, or other toxic results from your spouse's actions or behaviors.

Document incidents in a journal or calendar. Make notes in a journal or calendar of the details, dates, and times of all incidents that show a pattern of behavior. Also, note any failure-to-meet agreements, such as missed visitation or late pick-ups or drop-offs of children, bills not paid, temporary support not paid, sale of assets, or account withdrawals. Include the names of any others who were present and whether or not you have evidence.

Physical/Emotional Symptoms

If your marriage has been toxic or abusive, you have already suffered enough. Chronic stress and emotional abuse can cause serious damage. Please document any changes you have noticed in yourself, such as depression, anxiety, insomnia, panic attacks, or ruminating or obsessive thoughts. Report these symptoms to your physician and your therapist so they have a record of how long and how severely you have been impacted.

Just as you are gathering evidence and documenting your spouse's behavior, it's likely that they are doing the same. As noted earlier, vent to your friends, your coach, your therapist, or your doctor, but keep your cool with your partner. Do not give them anything that could be used against you at a later time.

BUILDING A SUPPORT NETWORK

High-conflict divorce isn't just a battle, it's also a marathon. It can take a tremendous emotional and physical toll on you, so you'll want to employ a variety of resources so you can stay strong, supported, and protected.

Life goes on during divorce. You have a job to go to, children or parents to care for, or volunteer activities to attend. Simple tasks like paying the bills or keeping food on the table can become daunting when life is so topsy-turvy.

Even if you're "used to" a tense or tumultuous marriage, the coping mechanisms you developed during your marriage will need to be stepped up to withstand the new pressures and tactics that will be hurled your way during high-conflict divorce. Now more than ever before, it will benefit you to build and rely on a network of friends, family, and professionals to advise you and stand by you.

Don't be afraid to ask for support. People close to you want to help—sometimes they just don't know how.

The BFF Backup

Who's going to be your go-to in all of this? It could be your mom, your sister, a friend, or a trusted neighbor. Someone who knows your whole truth, has a key to your house, is on the pick-up list to get your kids from school, and can see you with bed hair. This may be the person you are using for your safe storage or to provide emergency shelter if needed. This person is your BFF Backup. And yes, you can have more than one.

You need at least one person who can be there for you when you can't. Your BFF Backup will ideally know you well enough that you may not even have to ask—they already know and will step in. And they can help coordinate with your next team member, the Taskmaster.

The Taskmaster

When times of trouble hit, many people will say "What can I do?" or "Let me know if you need anything." This is the friend who means it and knows how to get things done. They may not be the friend who's going to sit with you for hours listening to tales of woe, but when it's time for action, they are on the job.

This person may love to go online and find things out. They will spend hours helping you research attorneys and places to live, find a realtor, look up divorce laws, drop off, pick up, make copies, organize files, grocery shop, and so on. Take a look at your to-do list and delegate anything you possibly can. Their love language is acts of service, so let them love you that way.

Support Groups

Support groups, both in person and online, can help you feel less alone, connect you with others who can relate, provide you with practical information and resources, and support you in healing and recovery.

If you were married to an abusive or controlling partner, they may have isolated you from friends and family, making this journey even more lonely. Or perhaps some of your friends and family are having a hard time believing that your "we always liked them so much" partner is really doing the things you are telling them. That can feel like abandonment on top of betrayal.

So, where can you turn to find others who have gone through the same experience? Who won't think you're crazy? Who will trust that what you say is true and validate the emotions you're feeling? The answer is women's divorce support groups.

There you'll find a sisterhood of women with the same wounds and fears who speak the same language. An instant bond develops between women who are vulnerable enough to share their deepest, darkest thoughts, ask for help, and listen to each other's pain.

Support groups are available for other issues as well. If you have been struggling with alcohol or other addictions, now is the time to start getting serious help for those. Your partner will try to use this against you; however, the courts will look more favorably on you when you can show you are actively taking measures to get better. You want to be able to show 12-step attendance, a sponsor, and a good period of sobriety.

No matter the support you need, do some Internet research to find a group that's right for you, or check the Resources section (page 185) for recommendations.

Divorce Coach/Therapist

A certified divorce coach can benefit you in many ways. They can provide the practical assistance you need to prepare for and navigate the process of divorce. Your coach can also help you understand and manage your emotional reactions so you can stay on the high road for your sake as well as that of your children. They can act as a sounding board to help you clarify your goals and priorities and support you each step of the way through the divorce process.

A therapist can offer insight into your partner's toxic behavior and how you can best insulate yourself and your children from it. A therapist can also assist you in finding solutions to stubborn or cyclic personal or family issues, and identify if you are suffering from any mental health concerns that need to be addressed. Again, your partner may try to use mental health issues against you, so it can be helpful to be able to tell the judge that you have been in treatment if you need to defend yourself against allegations of being unfit.

Physician

A visit to your doctor may be in order if you're feeling run-down, having trouble sleeping, feel your heart racing, or just generally don't feel like yourself. Your family doctor or general practitioner can be a valuable support resource. They have heard and seen others in your situation and can offer medical options and resource recommendations. If you need medication as part of a treatment plan to address a physical or mental health concern, be sure that you are getting it. Not only will you feel better and be more able to cope with the stress of divorce, but the judge will see it as a favorable reflection on you.

HOW TO TELL, WHO TO TELL

Once divorce becomes a reality, it will be time to decide who to tell and what to tell them. High-conflict divorce requires you to be protective, even a little paranoid, about how much you share.

Have you heard the phrase, "anything you say can and will be used against you in a court of law"? This is called the Miranda warning. You may have heard this warning given to criminal suspects when taken into custody or being interrogated. However, it can also apply to an upstanding, innocent person who is stuck in a high-conflict divorce. Keep this phrase in mind when choosing what details of your divorce to discuss and with whom.

Unfortunately, many people love to gossip, and the version of the story they repeat may bear no resemblance to the original. And if your spouse is a charmer, they can manipulate people into sharing information, especially if you had mutual friends or acquaintances.

Think of the details of your divorce like bars of precious gold you have stored in a bank vault. You are only going to give the vault combination to your most trustworthy allies. Having a strong support network will give you safe places to share and can prevent you from blurting out the vault combination to people who don't deserve access.

When in doubt, share less, not more.

Scripts

One strategy that works really well for sharing the news of your divorce is pre-planned scripts, which you can memorize and use whenever you need to talk about your situation. It eliminates the stress and panic of being put on the spot and fumbling for the right words. A little advance planning will protect you from sharing too little or too much, or saying things you don't mean to say or that aren't in your best legal interest when you run into someone at the grocery store. It also gives you the strength to deflect questions from people who are prying or trying to tell you what to do.

Check out **What to Say When** (page 23) for ideas for specific scripts, but never hesitate to pull out one of the two mother scripts:

"I'd prefer not to talk about it."

"I'm sorry, but my lawyer advised me not to discuss it."

You don't owe anyone an explanation for why you're doing what you're doing, no matter how much they pressure you.

A Quick Warning About Social Media

Social media records are used as evidence in 30 to 40 percent of divorce cases, which means that discussing your divorce with friends and family should be done in private and in person only. Under no circumstance should you post or message anyone about your divorce, your spouse, or their affair partner, as satisfying as the idea might feel in your head.

If you think you might need to use evidence from social media in your case, screenshot, download, or print everything as soon as you see it, before it disappears or gets blocked.

Consider shutting down or hiding your social media accounts while you are in the process of divorce. Block your spouse and any of their friends, accomplices, and toxic family members. This is especially critical if you have many mutual friends and acquaintances. Lock your accounts so everything is set to private and is seen by "only you." Go back and limit privacy on past posts, too. Your spouse might try to use even the most innocent photos you post to accuse you of partying irresponsibly, seeing someone else, or neglecting your children.

Family/Friends

Family and friends will probably be asking lots of questions. The level to which you want to share with them is something only you can decide.

Before you open up, ask yourself: Are they safe? Do they have your back? Are they non-judgmental and empathetic listeners? Or is there a chance they could share information with your partner because they're "still friends" with them? Do they tell you what to do, demand things, or criticize your actions?

If your family member or friend is safe, supportive, and nontoxic, you may not need a script. You may be able to share freely and openly without fear that you will be attacked or thrown under the bus. However, there still may be times that you just don't feel like talking or need to keep things private.

If you're not sure they're going to be on your team, you might choose to share at a high level (minimal details), but don't get too cozy or trusting.

A note about "Switzerland friends." There will be those people who just *loooove* both of you and will tell you that they want to remain friends with both you and your partner. Beware. Especially in high-conflict divorce, you cannot afford to take a chance that something you tell them in confidence will get repeated to your partner.

Employer/Teachers/Acquaintances

These are people that are not in your inner circle and don't need access to details. That, of course, doesn't prevent some from being nosy or asking personal questions.

You may want to let your employer or your children's teachers know, in general, what you are going through just so they can be on the lookout for your spouse and understand any differences in your performance/children's behavior. Something as simple as, *"I just wanted to let you know that I am going through a particularly difficult divorce right now. There is quite a bit of conflict and stress. I will do my best not to let it impact my performance/children, but I wanted to make you aware."*

Acquaintances like mothers of your children's teammates, your grandma's friend, your hairdresser, or your second cousin twice-removed can get a standard, noncommittal script like, *"Yes, we are divorcing, and I am hoping to keep it a private matter."*

WHAT TO SAY WHEN

Rehearsed scripts will help you address questions or deflect comments from friends, family, and acquaintances. Whether you aren't in the right frame of mind, the person is being inappropriate, or you simply don't feel safe with them, consider these responses:

"I'm feeling a little overwhelmed and need to take a break from talking about this."

"I love you and appreciate you caring about me, but I need to keep those details private."

"I'm not prepared to talk about that with you right now."

"This is really difficult for me and the children, and talking about it is hard for me. I hope you will understand."

"Yes, we are divorcing, and I'm really not ready to share any more than that."

"I really can't respond to that."

"You may not know the whole story, so I would appreciate if you didn't repeat that."

"This is a private matter, and I'd prefer to keep it that way."

"I appreciate your support."

And remember, when in doubt, never hesitate to use the mother scripts:

"I'd prefer not to talk about it."

"I'm sorry, but my lawyer advised me not to discuss it."

CHAPTER TWO

GETTING YOUR LEGAL AFFAIRS IN ORDER

Two things cause the most conflict in divorce—kids and money. And getting an equitable financial outcome, especially in high-conflict divorce, depends on proper legal and financial preparation. You can do some of the legwork yourself by gathering documents and running numbers, but you will want to enlist the services of experts to ensure your rights are protected.

PREPARING THE PAPERWORK

Divorce means paperwork, and lots of it.

The first step in getting ready to file or respond to your partner's filing is to gather all the documentation you can, make copies, and save them in your safe storage location. But where to start?

Here is a list of documents that may be required. It can look intimidating, especially if you've not been actively involved in your family finances, but don't panic. If you can't find all of them or don't have access, there is a later step in the divorce process called "discovery," when you can legally compel the other side to provide copies of anything else you need:

- Individual income tax returns (federal, state, local) for past three years
- Business income tax returns (federal, state, local) for past three years
- Proof of your current income (paystubs, statements, or paid invoices)
- Proof of spouse's income (paystubs, statements, or paid invoices)
- Checking, savings, and certificate statements (personal and business) for past three years
- Credit card and loan statements (personal and business) for past three years
- Investment, pension plan, and retirement account statements for past three years
- Mortgage statement and loan documents for all properties you have an interest in

- Real estate appraisals
- Property tax documents
- Employment contracts
- Benefit statements
- Social Security statements
- Life, homeowner's, and auto insurance policies
- Wills and trust agreements
- Health insurance cards
- Vehicle titles and/or registration
- Monthly budget worksheet
- List of personal property (furnishings, jewelry, electronics, artwork)
- List of property acquired by gift or inheritance or owned prior to marriage
- Prenuptial agreements
- Marriage license
- Prior court orders directing payment of child support or spousal support

Your attorney or financial advisor may ask for additional documents specific to your case. Some of these may not be applicable to you. Every divorce is unique, with its own financial circumstances.

GETTING YOUR FINANCES IN ORDER

Much of the divorce process is about breaking a legal contract and dividing up your financial life—assets, debt, spousal support, and child support. We'll walk through some of the information you will be asked to produce.

Financial Affidavit

Both you and your spouse will be asked to submit a financial statement to the court.

Forms in each state are different and they go by different names, but the basic information is the same. These forms give judges the information necessary to make fair decisions on child support, alimony, and division of assets and debts. Your attorney should be able to provide you with a copy of your local form, and most domestic relations courts have them available online to download.

Your financial statements need to be accurate to ensure an equitable division, and in a high-conflict divorce, that becomes even more important. Your spouse is doing everything they can to get you to agree to an unfair and unbalanced settlement. Your best defense is proper documentation of assets, debts, income, and expenses.

Financial disclosure serves two important purposes in divorce:

First, it is a legal instrument intended to compel both parties to accurately disclose financial data. Chances are that your high-conflict partner may try to delay, omit information, or otherwise hinder what should be a simple, straightforward process.

Susan was a victim of this tactic:

"He hid a lot of income to avoid paying support on it and he didn't disclose significant bonuses. He was scheduled for a 30 percent raise right before our hearing and had his company defer it until after the divorce was final so that his support payments wouldn't be adjusted upward."

Second, these forms will be used as the basis for negotiation and decision-making. If you don't accurately assess your true financial picture, you could be awarded, or agree to, less than you need or deserve.

Marital Lifestyle Analysis

One of the best places to start gathering the information you will need for your financial affidavit is reviewing your previous marital lifestyle; that is, the income and expenses that were part of your life during your marriage.

Gather six to 12 months of checking, savings, and credit card statements, and break your income and expenses down into categories and then line items. I have suggested some here, but add your own as needed.

Check to see if your bank or credit card company provides reporting that categorizes charges or lets you assign categories—your work may already be almost done for you:

- Income—paychecks, interest, dividends, rents, royalties, business income, pension, social security, child support, spousal support

- Housing—mortgage/rent, property taxes, HOA dues, insurance
- Utilities—gas, electric, propane, phone, TV/Internet, trash, water/sewer
- Food—groceries, dining out
- Auto—car payments, gasoline, repairs, insurance
- Medical—health insurance, doctor/dentist visits, prescriptions, physical therapy
- Entertainment—travel, concerts/shows, sports
- Clothing—personal purchases, dry cleaning, uniforms
- Personal care—hair/nails, gym/yoga, vitamins/supplements
- Miscellaneous—gifts, pets, donations
- Children—education, activities, school lunches, childcare

You can use a spreadsheet or pen and paper to take note of income and expenses as you go through statements, then calculate a monthly average for each item.

Be on the lookout for unusual withdrawals, transfers, deposits, or cash advances, and document those for your attorney. Also keep an eye out for expenses that don't occur regularly, like property taxes, insurance premiums, tax preparation fees, tuition, professional association dues, and so on. You don't want to forget to include them in the expense section of your financial disclosure.

Post-Divorce Budget

Your post-divorce lifestyle may look very different from how you lived when you were married. The income that covered expenses for one household may not stretch as far paying for two separate sets of bills.

Look back at your marital lifestyle analysis and see what adjustments might need to be made for your post-divorce life.

- Where will you live?
- What expenses will change?
- Will you be receiving child support or spousal support (maintenance)?
- Are you planning to return to work, get additional training, or make a career change?
- How close are you to retirement age?

Nobody can predict the future perfectly. But you can make an educated guess about what kind of cash flow it will take to cover your living expenses post-divorce.

If you've been a stay-at-home parent or are earning a lot less than your spouse, I know this can be intimidating when you first look at the numbers. This is where we have to live in truth and create a plan to earn more or spend less to make the budget balance.

I want you to understand that knowledge is power. Your spouse may have no idea you are gathering all this information and financial literacy, and that will serve you well in the courtroom. Let your ex underestimate you.

It can be helpful to play around with different scenarios to see the impact of different decisions.

For example:

- What if you sell the house?
- What if you take a lump sum instead of monthly spousal support payments?
- What if you take more of the debt in exchange for more retirement assets?
- What if you work 30 hours a week instead of 20?

A little resourceful thinking can help open the door to different possibilities. And possibilities help to diminish fear and increase confidence and faith in what the future may hold for you.

The Role of the Financial Advisor

The more money that's involved, the more important it becomes to have the right financial professional involved in your case. If your finances are fairly simple, you may not require the services of a specialized financial pro.

But if you or your spouse own multiple properties, are self-employed, run cash-based businesses, own trusts, have assets from inheritances, or have complicated retirement accounts, stock options, or pensions, then a full-service financial advisor with a CDFA® (Certified Divorce Financial Analyst) designation may be well worth the investment.

RIGHTS AND OPTIONS

Since the introduction of no-fault divorce, women now have the right to divorce their partners without proving a legal case, like adultery or abuse, or requiring their spouse's approval.

The good news is that women can now end their marriages to abusive, high-conflict, or otherwise dysfunctional partners by filing for no-fault divorce, and neither their spouse nor the judge can deny them the right to divorce.

Along with no-fault divorce, there have been other changes in more recent years. Modern law treats each gender and each parent equally in terms of property distribution, parenting time, custody, child support, and spousal support.

No longer does the stay-at-home parent automatically get full custody or decades of spousal support. Many judges rule in favor of shared custody. Now more than ever, you need to be prepared to support any requests you are making to differ from the 50/50 parenting and rehabilitative spousal support defaults that may be in place.

UNDERSTANDING YOUR STATE'S DIVORCE LAW

Laws governing divorce are determined by each individual state, so although they cover the same basic concepts, there are some important differences. The set of statutes your divorce will be subject to is based on the state in which the divorce is filed.

To research your local divorce statutes, do an Internet search for "_____ state divorce laws" and find your local bar association or county resources. For a general overview and easy-to-read summary, check out DivorceSource.com or MaritalLaws.com and just click on your state.

Note that Internet sources can be helpful to begin understanding how divorce works in your state, but will not replace individual, professional legal guidance.

Legal Components of Divorce

In general, divorce means establishing a legal agreement about the following four items:

1. Property distribution (assets, debts, and household goods)
2. Child custody
3. Child support
4. Spousal support

Although divorce law is complex and varies from state to state, there are certain common elements that you will want to know:

Separation requirements

- How long must you and your partner be living separate and apart before you can file for divorce? Before divorce can be granted?
- What is the definition of "separate and apart"?

Residency requirements

- How long must you be a resident of your state (and perhaps your county/jurisdiction) to file for divorce there?

Community property or equitable distribution

- Community property states split all marital property 50/50.
- Equitable distribution states can choose an allocation other than 50/50 based on a number of factors.

Marital or separate property

- Property (home, retirement account, furniture) you owned before the marriage, as well as some gifts and inheritances, can be considered your separate property and therefore not be subject to division.
- State laws differ as to their definitions and requirements that something is separate property.

Parenting/Custody

- Does your state have any standard custody or visitation guidelines, and what is required to vary from those guidelines?
- Is a parenting plan required? What is included in the parenting agreement?

THE IMPORTANCE OF RETAINING A LAWYER

Divorce is, at its core, a legal matter. It is the breaking of a legal contract between two individuals. High-conflict divorce almost always requires a lawyer because of the adversarial behavior of your spouse and your need for protection.

But do you need to have an attorney to divorce? No, you don't. However, in any divorce and even more so in high-conflict divorce, trying to navigate your way through the jungle of rules, laws, deadlines, clerks, magistrates, and judges could easily overwhelm anyone and leave you vulnerable.

Unfortunately, divorce law isn't simple, and the rules that one must follow to file all the paperwork are complex. Many statutes are written such that each individual judge has leeway as to how they interpret and apply certain sections of the law. If you aren't familiar with the process and people in your local domestic relations court, you could be fighting two uphill battles at the same time: your partner *and* the court system.

In many states, there is no calculation to determine spousal support. It is up to you to make your case. An experienced family law attorney knows what is typical in cases like yours, and what evidence you need to make the strongest case.

Keep in mind, your spouse will probably not play nice or even play by the rules. A fellow divorce coach shared this story of a former client:

"Dad took a video of mom napping on the couch. He sent it to the children, saying that mom was drunk and passed out (which was not true). He used it against her in court in order to avoid paying child support. He was awarded full custody of the children and she was ordered to go to rehab for alcoholism. A year and a half later, the children have figured out the truth and live with mom, but she still receives no child support."

This is an extreme case, but the point is that having someone who knows their way around divorce law and who can anticipate what needs to happen next is a must in high-conflict divorce. You need a lawyer who can protect you. There's too much at stake to go in unarmed and uneducated.

HOW TO CHOOSE A LAWYER

We've explored some of the advantages of having an attorney on your team in a high-conflict divorce, but how do you go about choosing the right one for you?

First, no two divorces are the same. Just because your Aunt Susie or friend Joan was satisfied with their attorney doesn't mean they will be the best fit for you. Personal recommendations are just one factor to consider.

Ask around in your support group. Ask friends and family. Ask other professionals for referrals. Check on Avvo.com or SuperLawyers.com for family law specialists in your area. Many attorneys offer a free consultation, so I recommend that you plan to interview at least three before you make a choice. If lawyers in your area charge a consultation fee, see if you can get a few of the following questions answered before you decide to make a consultation appointment.

Note: Don't procrastinate this step. One common dirty divorce tactic is for your spouse to book consultations with all the best attorneys in town so they are "conflicted out" from being able to represent you.

Questions to Ask

When interviewing potential attorneys, you want to be assured that they are a family law specialist, not a jack-of-all-legal-trades. You also need to assess their level of experience with high-conflict divorce and personality disorders.

Here are some questions to determine if this attorney has the experience to represent you well:

What percentage of your practice/caseload is family law?

Ideally, this should be 100 percent. You want someone who spends the majority of their time focused on divorce and divorce-related matters.

How many divorce cases have you represented in my county/ jurisdiction in the past 12 months?

Judges in each jurisdiction can rule quite differently, even though state law is consistent. You want to make sure that your attorney is very familiar with the judges in your specific area and how their courts run.

What is your experience in high-conflict divorce cases, and how does your approach differ when dealing with these cases?

Listen for their understanding of personality disorders like narcissism, discussion of extra protective orders or measures, stories of previous cases, and successful actions they took or outcomes they had.

Have you had to mount a defense against false abuse, addiction, or child neglect accusations? Were you successful? How did you handle it?

Again, you want to hear them demonstrate that they have a deep understanding of the evil you could be up against, and that they have actual experience with a case like yours and had a successful outcome.

Listen for indication that they are willing to support you in mediation and are a strong negotiator, since 95 percent of cases settle without going to court (even high-conflict ones), and that saves money. But you will also want to hear that they have trial experience and aren't intimidated by the prospect of having to argue in court.

In addition, you'll want to understand how you will be billed, so you can manage your costs and not have any nasty surprises. And finally, you need to get a feel for how accessible and responsive you can expect your attorney to be. Are they easy to talk to? Are they sympathetic and responsive to your issues and concerns? Are they taking your questions seriously, and not dismissive or patronizing in any way? See **What to Say When** (page 45) for more questions to ask when seeking the right attorney.

COMMON GROUNDS FOR FILING FOR DIVORCE

On what grounds are you filing for divorce? At one time, you had to have photos from a private eye showing adultery or a police report proving domestic violence (including marital rape) in order to be granted a divorce.

Thanks to the introduction of no-fault divorce in California in 1970, those days are behind us.

No-Fault Divorce

Every state in the US now has some provision for no-fault divorce. This means that nobody is required to prove fault on the part of the other person. You can simply get divorced on the basis of "irreconcilable differences" or "irretrievable break-down of the marriage."

Be aware, however, that some states do have separation requirements, meaning that you must live separately for a period of time (and perhaps attend counseling) before you can file for no-fault divorce.

A spouse cannot refuse or object to their partner's filing for a no-fault divorce. No-fault divorce is very common and typically results in less tension, less antagonism, lower legal costs, and a faster overall divorce process.

Fault-Based Divorce

In states that allow it, some people still choose to file for divorce on at-fault grounds because:

1. Their state provides some sort of advantage to the not-at-fault spouse for division of property or custody.
2. The mandatory separation period can be avoided.
3. They are a high-conflict person who loves to fight.

Again, each state has its own language and its own fault grounds, but here are a few of the most common:

- Adultery
- Abandonment (desertion)
- Extreme cruelty (physical or mental)
- Substance abuse

- Long-term imprisonment
- Mental illness/insanity (incurable)
- Sexual issues

The petitioner (or person filing) must prove to the court that their spouse is responsible for the breakdown of the marriage as a result of the "fault" or reason claimed in the divorce filing. However, your spouse is able to present a defense against your claim and, if successful in convincing the judge that they were not at fault, the judge may choose not to grant the divorce.

So, there is a risk/reward proposition in filing for at-fault divorce. On the one hand, you may get a larger portion of the marital property, more spousal support, or greater custody, but you could also spend all that time and money just to have your divorce request denied and have to start all over.

WAYS TO FILE FOR DIVORCE

Next, I'll outline the various options you have for negotiating and filing for your divorce. As a divorce professional, I must tell you that I don't recommend going through high-conflict divorce without some sort of legal professional on your team— I'll explain some of those pitfalls in each section.

Even if you and your partner agree to everything, I cannot stress strongly enough that you should hire your own attorney to give your agreement the once-over before signing it. The stakes are too high to leave yourself unprotected.

Beware the perils of "sharing" a lawyer with your partner. If your partner has hired that lawyer, that lawyer is legally obligated to protect your partner's interests, not yours.

Pro Se

This is the do-it-yourself version. You'll represent yourself with no legal counsel. You are responsible for filing your own paperwork with the court and documenting the terms of your settlement agreement.

You and your partner can agree to the terms and complete the paperwork, or you alone can file for divorce.

If you file for divorce and represent yourself pro se, you will also be required to follow court procedures, meet deadlines, and could even end up presenting your own case in front of the judge. You can retain an attorney at any point if the research or legalese becomes too much.

Because you don't know what you don't know about the law, I believe that pro se should be a last resort for anyone in a high-conflict situation.

Online Divorce

Today, there are a variety of options for preparing your divorce paperwork online. Keep in mind, only a judge can sign the order to end your marriage, so you aren't getting divorced, just getting support to fill out the forms correctly. Services range from a few hundred dollars to several thousand, depending on the level of support you choose.

Online divorce, like pro se, is best for uncontested cases where the two of you plan to work out your own agreement and then use the service to guide you through completing the required forms. Once again, this is probably not going to be in your best interest in a high-conflict divorce.

Mediation

You and your partner can hire and work directly with a private, professional mediator to facilitate your discussions and negotiations. Mediation can be conducted pro se or with the guidance of an attorney. If there has been a power imbalance in the marriage, some women can be reluctant to participate in mediation. However, proper support and preparation from a divorce coach or attorney can sometimes make you feel confident enough to negotiate on your own behalf.

Mediation is often considered a better alternative for high-conflict cases, since professional mediators are trained in conflict resolution. Mediation may keep your conflict from turning into combat. Especially when children are involved, divorcing couples who learn conflict resolution skills have a better chance of being effective co-parents.

Arbitration

Arbitration is similar to mediation; however, if there are issues the two of you can't resolve, you agree that the arbiter (usually a judge) will make a final and binding decision.

Collaborative Divorce

Collaborative divorce is a process in which both sides agree not to go to trial. Typically, you each have an attorney, and a variety of other professional neutrals assist with your case: financial advisors, parenting coordinators, divorce coaches. You all work together to come to an agreement. If you aren't able to resolve your differences and decide to go the trial route, each of you must begin the process again with a new lawyer.

When this process works, it can be valuable, and like mediation, helps retain the co-parenting relationship between the couple. When it doesn't work, it is extremely expensive and time-consuming.

Attorney-Led/Litigation

If you believe that you and your partner won't be able to come to an agreement on your own, either with a mediator or through a collaborative process, then using the traditional attorney-led process may be best for you.

Using an attorney doesn't necessarily mean you will go to trial. Nearly all cases are settled, often through discussions between the opposing attorneys and in consultation with magistrates and judges. It is only if you are unable to come to agreement on one or more issues that you would actually go to court, present your case, and ask the judge to make a ruling.

This can be the most time-consuming and expensive option. Yet, it can sometimes be the only option for women who need to protect themselves in high-conflict divorce. It's what some women might call "the cost of freedom."

WHAT TO SAY WHEN

You now know what questions to ask to determine that a particular attorney has the expertise to handle your case. But there is nothing more frustrating than feeling like your attorney isn't there for you or getting a bill that is thousands more than you were expecting. You are putting your future in this person's hands, so do your due diligence to understand how they operate. Here are a few other questions just to be sure your expectations are clear:

- What is your current caseload? How available are you?
- What is your retainer fee?
- How do you bill for your services?
- What is the best way to communicate with you, and how quickly can I expect a reply?
- Will you be the only one working on my case, or will others, such as paralegals, be involved?
- How often do you expect that we will meet or talk to discuss my case?
- Will all decisions regarding my case be sent through me for approval?
- What can I do to make sure I utilize your services as efficiently as possible?

CHAPTER THREE

EXPLAINING DIVORCE TO CHILDREN

If you're like most parents, one of your main concerns about the divorce process is your children. You are determined to protect them as best you can from the conflict and do everything in your power to help them adapt and thrive after divorce. High-conflict divorce has some special challenges, but you can set yourself and your children up for a better outcome by planning ahead.

HOW TO TELL YOUR CHILDREN

Telling your children about the divorce can feel intimidating. *What will they think? How will they react? Will they blame us for ruining their lives? Will they pick sides?*

Children are perceptive. Even young children are probably more aware of the tension and conflict in your marriage than you realize. Trying to hide the truth from them creates anxiety. The best thing you can do for them is to be honest in an age-appropriate manner. Honesty helps put them at ease that what they've been feeling is real, and it builds trust that you will be straightforward with them.

All children need to know three things when their parents are divorcing:

1. You're safe.
2. We will always be a family.
3. We both love you.

Best Practice

In an ideal world, both parents sit down together with the children and tell them about the divorce. They display a united front to the children and don't blame or bad-mouth each other. It's still painful, but the kids are reassured that none of this is their fault, and questions are answered as honestly and thoughtfully as possible.

This approach provides children of all ages with the sense that their family is changing, but not disintegrating. Older children may have friends whose parents went through ugly divorces; maybe the parents still fight, or one parent moved away. A united approach will give them hope that your divorce won't be that way.

Of course, preschool-level communication won't satisfy a high schooler, and high school discussions won't be helpful for a preschooler, so let older children know that you plan to have follow-up conversations with them at a later time—and then, make a date to follow through on that promise.

No Secrets/No Lies

You might feel like you want to protect younger children from any discussion of divorce in the early stages. Telling the older kids but asking them to keep secrets from their younger siblings is asking them to carry an unfair burden.

Trust and transparency are so important for maintaining healthy relationships with your children. Try your best to foster an environment where honesty and authenticity are valued. This means telling the truth, as well as not promising things you may not be able to deliver on, such as:

- We will still live in this house.
- Dad will take you to dinner three nights a week.
- Our family pet will always live here with you.
- You'll never have to spend the night at dad's with his girl-friend and her kids.
- Nothing will change.

High-Conflict Complications

When parents cannot present a united front, which is typical in high-conflict divorce, you have no control over and may not even know the details of the story your partner is telling the children.

Susan had to help her children recover from this bomb when she told her abusive husband that she wanted a divorce:

> "He called the three kids into the room and said, 'Kids, your mother doesn't love me anymore and wants a divorce. I'll be moving far away and probably won't see you anymore. You can thank her for this.'"

Parental alienation tactics can begin early, and your spouse may start planting seeds with your kids that you are the "bad" one, or you are to blame for the breakup. Your children may repeat hurtful, untrue things they've heard their other parent say.

As tempting as it will be to counter-argue or come back with stories about your partner, hold on tight. Ignoring it is the best strategy at this point. Keep taking the high road and doing what's best for your children. If you feel you must speak up, keep your words short and sweet: "Thank you for letting me know that. It isn't true, and I hope you know how much I love you and that I always try my best to be a good parent. Is there anything else you would like to know?"

You may also want to document any particularly damaging, untrue, or inflammatory comments you hear from your spouse or through your children in your private journal or calendar.

What Children Need to Know

Although children at different ages are able to grasp varying levels of what divorce means, it's best to keep all conversations brief, direct, and factual. Children don't need to hear what caused the breakup or a recitation of all your partner's character flaws.

There may be a later time to be more transparent about the reasons for the divorce, but this conversation is not the place. The purpose of this first conversation is to inform them that the divorce is happening, let them know how much you care for them, make them feel safe, and discuss any details you have sorted out about living and visitation arrangements.

These are shatteringly difficult conversations, and your first reaction is to want to take your child's pain away, but pat answers or reassurances like "it will be okay" or "things will be fine" aren't helpful. Everyone knows that things are going to be different, and these types of responses can make children feel like their anxieties are being dismissed.

The goal here should be to give age-appropriate information and reassurances. Younger children typically require more discussion around security, that mom and dad both love them and that they are not to blame in any way. Older children may be more concerned about living arrangements and how their social life will be impacted. They may also have been expecting it, and in cases where marital conflict was high, they may even find it a relief.

Primary Concerns/Needs by Age

Infants/Toddlers: Ages 0 to 2

Babies, of course, will not understand that you're divorcing. The best way you can reassure them during the transition is to provide calmness, consistency, and stability in their caregiving and their routines.

Because they are completely dependent on you for all their needs, little ones are very attuned to your emotional state. The more you can keep yourself settled, the less upset your infant is likely to be.

Preschool: Ages 3 to 5

Many preschoolers' favorite words are "me" and "no." Their view of the world is that it revolves around them, and all messages get filtered through that lens. At this age, children only need to know that their parents will be living apart, they will spend time with both of them, and they are very loved.

They have a limited ability to understand what you are telling them, so keep your messages short and be ready to repeat conversations about the same topics. Think of the four-year-old who asks "why?" 50 times a day and is never satisfied with any answer—they just keep asking.

Elementary: Ages 6 to 8

At this age, children have started forming friendships at school and are beginning to get the idea of what being in a relationship with someone means. However, their life still primarily revolves around their family and the security they get from it. A loss of security may make them take one parent's side or harbor fantasies about their parents getting back together.

You can help by reminding them how much you love them, and providing information about changes to where they will live, visitation schedules, and when they will see each of their parents. You may need to reaffirm that you will not be getting back together and reassure them that they haven't done anything to cause the divorce.

Preteens: Ages 9 to 12

Many preteens like to think they are adults and want to be treated that way. Although preteens have a better understanding of complex issues and likely have a realistic view of divorce, they still tend to think in absolutes—right or wrong. They may feel very torn between their parents.

Try to listen to them nonjudgmentally. Reassure your preteen that you love them and that it's okay to love both parents and you don't want them to choose sides. Explain the logistical details (such as living arrangements), and let them know that you will do your best to keep them protected from any adult issues.

Teens: Ages 13 to 18

Despite their growing sense of independence, teenagers haven't lost their need for their parents. They have a much deeper ability to understand the issues related to divorce and may even have experienced their own breakups. If they already have a troubled relationship with one parent, the divorce could cause even more damage.

Their concerns may center around how the changes will affect their schedule and ability to conduct their lives as usual. They may also have financial concerns as perhaps they are looking forward to college, or worrying where you will live. To the best of your ability, give them straightforward information about why you're divorcing and what changes they can expect.

Check out **What to Say When** (page 64) for tips on how you can answer some questions children commonly ask about divorce.

WAYS CHILDREN REACT

There are as many different reactions to divorce as there are personalities of children. The inquisitive ones may speak up right away and ask questions. Others may storm out, cry, or seem to have no reaction at all. Some children will try to "fix" things. Adjustment will be an ongoing process, as new schedules and routines get established.

If your child is threatening to harm themselves or others, please get help immediately. Call 911, the National Suicide Prevention Lifeline at 1-800-273-TALK (8255), or the National Domestic Violence Hotline at 1-800-799-SAFE (7233).

Children can have intense reactions to any divorce. Any divorce, especially high-conflict divorce, can be extremely traumatic for them. Almost all children can benefit from the support of a trained therapist. This can be critical if you are worried about their safety or emotional well-being when in the care of their other parent. A therapist is an excellent sounding board for any concerns. Here your child will have a safe space to share, and the therapist is obligated to report to authorities if they hear anything distressing.

With any age child, the best thing you can do is be observant. Watch for signs of distress, and get specialized help right away if your child seems to be having adjustment problems.

Changes You May Observe

Some common reactions and changes you may notice:

Regression: Younger children who have been potty trained, are sleeping through the night, or have stopped sucking their thumbs may revert back to earlier behaviors.

Clinginess/Separation anxiety: Children may be reluctant to be without you, go to childcare or school, or visit their other parent. Younger ones may worry when you are out of sight at home.

Sleep problems/Nightmares: Emotions can manifest at nighttime. Children may ask to sleep with a light on or sleep with you in order to feel a sense of safety.

Disinterest: Some children may initially appear to be unfazed by or disinterested in the news of the divorce, but if it continues, notice if anything else appears to be off. They may be repressing their feelings of sadness or anger by denying that anything has changed.

Anger/Aggression: Many children will initially be angry about the split, but some will remain stuck in that anger and become aggressive with parents, siblings, and even friends. Aggression can escalate to verbal abuse, physical fighting, property destruction, running away, or other behaviors.

Sadness/Depression: Feelings of sadness are to be expected, but sadness can turn into depression, especially in teens. Symptoms of depression include fatigue, decreased interest in activities, changes in appetite or weight, sluggishness, feelings of worthlessness, trouble concentrating, and suicidal thoughts.

School difficulties: Children may begin to let their grades slip, fail to turn in assignments, get in trouble at school, or even skip school. They may begin to have trouble with friends from school and become more isolated.

Anxiety: Worrying about the changes that divorce will bring is normal; however, it can begin to cause problems. Symptoms of anxiety include restlessness, irritability, tiring easily, difficulty sleeping, trouble concentrating, and muscle tension. Anxiety can also cause diarrhea, sweating, and nausea.

How You Can Help

Children are especially sensitive to your stress and to changes in routine. Make every effort to manage your own emotions—if you are overly emotional, your children will be too. And while you may not have control over what happens at their other parent's home, you do have 100 percent control over what happens in yours. Create routines and consistency. Offer extra nurturing and comfort. Keep open channels of communication and maintain a positive environment. If tensions were high in your pre-divorce home, a commitment to peace can provide welcome comfort and relief to everyone, and set the stage for what a home should really be.

Teens and preteens can be especially hard to read, but frequent connection and communication will help you stay in touch with any emotional issues that may be simmering below their surface. Try not to let your own stress keep you from tuning in and spending time with older kids.

Helping Your Children Help Themselves

Resist your impulse to be the intermediary and fixer of all things. Your child has the right to love their imperfect other parent, and that relationship will be very different than the relationship you have with your partner. It's a big change for all of you. Your child will need to learn to communicate their needs and navigate on their own with the high-conflict parent.

In addition to surrounding your children with supportive, healthy adults (therapist, family members, guidance counselor, youth leader), you can begin to teach them age-appropriate information, not just about divorce, but also about subjects including sex, alcohol, drugs, and abuse. When we give our children knowledge, language, and agency, then they have the ability to make good decisions and speak up when something doesn't feel right to them.

Work to create an atmosphere of love and trust, where you are guiding your children to be informed and empowered. Invite them to ask you questions and tell you things. Listen without judgment. By doing so, you are helping them be healthier, more prepared, and more protected. You may not be able to run interference, but you can equip your children to be assertive, establish boundaries, and communicate when something is wrong.

MAKING YOUR CHILDREN YOUR PRIORITY

When you're in the middle of your own life-altering trauma, it can be helpful to have a road map to guide you when supporting your children through difficult times. This list, using the acronym PARENTS, comes from a grief specialist and dear friend of mine:

P—Process your pain first. Address your feelings as they come, so you can help your children manage their own emotions.

A—Ask them questions. Follow their level of curiosity. Keep in mind their level of understanding.

R—Respond with compassion toward their fears, anxiety, and confusion. Do not shame them or downplay their perspective.

E—Embrace them! Give hugs and physically reassure them of your presence.

N—Notice changes in behavior or outlook. If you need to, get help from a trusted friend, counselor, or pastor.

T—Tell the truth. Don't hide things from kids or lie to them. Don't tell them you are staying in the house or that your separation is temporary if it's not a fact. They can usually sense something is wrong, and ignoring it doesn't lower their stress level; it makes them more uneasy.

S—Stay on the high road. Keep children out of adult issues, and don't make disparaging remarks about their other parent.

Making your children your top priority means making decisions that are in their best interest, even when it's hard for you. This includes encouraging others around you to do the same. Your children need to be able to count on family members and other adults in their lives for support and not feel pressured to choose sides or discuss adult issues.

It is best that your kids:

- Be allowed to spend time with their other parent (if they are safe and healthy), regardless of how angry you may be
- Not be used to spy on your spouse, pass messages, or gather information
- Be able to love and talk about their other parent
- Have you as the safe, sane, stable parent, even when your partner is acting in a hateful way
- Not hear you say demeaning or disparaging things to them or others about their other parent
- Be able to be children and receive comfort from you, and not feel the need to provide emotional support for you
- Not have your adult issues impact their school, activities, or social life

MODELING HEALTHY BEHAVIOR

Modeling healthy behavior may be one of the most difficult things you will have to do during high-conflict divorce. You are incredibly stressed, have financial worries, are fighting for custody, and working hard to keep your head above water, and yet, your children need to see you modeling healthy behavior.

Does that mean you need to walk around whistling a tune and smiling from ear to ear? Absolutely not! Anger and sadness are real emotions, and hiding them from children does them a disservice. By showing them how you process those emotions in a healthy way, you're teaching them how to be healthy adults.

I know that you're angry. How could your partner do this to you? Some days that rage feels like it takes over. You want to blast your spouse on social media, key their car, or show up at their work and tell your story. Or maybe you want to scream at them on the phone or slug them with a baseball bat when they come to pick up the kids.

All of those might feel good, actually really good, for about 20 seconds. And then you'll see the look on your children's faces, or weeks later you'll hear them mimicking your behavior. Try to take the long view and remember this vitally important rule when you're frustrated:

No conflict between you and your soon-to-be-ex-partner should be greater than your children's needs.

So how do you model good behavior when you feel so bad? Read on.

Self-Care

Remember how the flight attendant says, "In the event of an emergency, place your own oxygen mask on first before assisting others"? That translates into parenting as well—if you are run-down, exhausted, and depleted, you cannot possibly care for anyone else.

If you really want to minimize the impact of high-conflict divorce on your children, then you need to grab that mask and take a big inhale. You can show your children how someone who is strong faces adversity by making certain that you are keeping yourself strong both physically and emotionally.

Physical Health

Taking care of your physical health includes eating right, getting some exercise, and allowing yourself plenty of restful sleep. I know making healthy meals may be the last thing you feel like doing at the end of a long day. Try being creative to come up with something that works for you, such as:

- Meal prep in batches and freeze ahead.
- Rotate limited menus.
- Keep easy-meal staples on hand, like whole-wheat pasta and grains, frozen veggies, and canned tuna, beans, and healthy soups.
- Breakfast for dinner. A quick pan of scrambled eggs or pancakes can feel quite comforting.
- Call your BFF Backup or Taskmaster and ask for help. Remember all those people who told you to let them know if you needed anything? Well, let them know. Groups put together what they call "meal trains" for folks who need a little extra help.

Other dietary choices that will benefit your health:

- Drink lots of water—fill and carry a reusable water bottle everywhere you go.
- Make smarter fast food choices and skip the soda.
- Take a multivitamin each day.

If you're having trouble sleeping, make changes to your routine that will help:

- Turn off screens 45 minutes before bed.
- Take a relaxing bath, listen to music, or read a light, enjoyable book.
- Try a fan, white noise machine, or guided meditation exercise.
- Make sure your room is dark and cool.

If nothing helps, talk with your doctor about other options to help you get better rest. You need sleep, and your children deserve a well-rested parent.

And finally, don't be too hard on yourself. Baby steps are still steps in the right direction.

Emotional Health

Caring for yourself emotionally means making sure you have the right support, a creative outlet, and some "you" time. It also means giving yourself permission to feel your feelings, not stifle it all, and process this hard stuff so you can continue on.

In the PARENTS process (page 58), you saw how important it is to process your own pain first. Name your feelings. Dig in and identify exactly what they are and where they are coming from. Did you know that many experts say that anger is a secondary emotion? That we choose anger because it feels powerful, and we would rather feel angry than the more vulnerable feelings underneath it. We would rather be mad than sad, afraid, rejected, ashamed, humiliated, guilty, or some other emotion that makes us feel weak or less-than. Learning to face and handle your own unpleasant feelings will give you back the power to be there for your children, and teach them how to handle hard things in life.

If you're struggling with your own emotions, reach out to a safe and trusted person who can help you, so you can support your children.

Scripts and Boundaries

When things get hard and you find yourself straining to model healthy behavior, you can always return to the safety of scripts and the natural boundaries they provide.

These scripts can help you remain calm and on the high road when talk of the other parent comes up. Again, adapt these to your situation or create your own.

If your child asks:

Mom/Dad says you're ruining our family. Is that true?

> Script: Our family will always be our family, and nothing can change that. We may live separately, but we'll still be your parents and love you the same.

Mom/Dad told me that you're trying to take all their money. Why are you doing that?

> Script: Your mom/dad and I are working that out between us. We have people helping us figure out what is fair for both of us.

Did you cheat? Did the other parent cheat? (By the nature of this question, your child is probably old enough to grasp the concept.)

> Script 1: Your other parent (mom/dad) and I got married and agreed to have a special relationship we didn't share with anyone else. Your mom/dad/I chose to have a

relationship with someone else and now I/they need to live separately to find a new way to be happy.

> Script 2: What happened between your dad/mom and I is an adult issue that I am not comfortable sharing with you because it doesn't have any effect on how much we love you or you love us.

In order to maintain your dignity and deserve the respect of your children, it's critical to remain civil about your partner at all times. You have a wonderful opportunity to teach them that they don't have to attend every fight they're invited to, and that mud-slinging is not required just because someone else is doing it. Modeling healthy behavior includes showing your children that you can keep your composure under pressure and hold your head high while under attack without retaliating.

As parents, we all want to shield our children from suffering, including the pain of divorce. One of the gifts we can give our children is to demonstrate how to cope effectively with uncomfortable and painful feelings. As hard as it may be, they will become better grown-ups for having learned that lesson.

WHAT TO SAY WHEN

Two things to keep in mind when answering questions or addressing comments from your children: Be honest and don't give false hope. They are going through enough change right now, and the one thing they need to be able to depend on is that they can trust you.

Don't you love my other parent anymore? Why not?
Say: Mom/Dad and I both love you so much, we'll still be your parents, and we'll still be a family. We aren't happy together, and we will be better parents if we can find our own happiness.

Why can't you just fight less?
Say: I wish we could, too. We just disagree on some really big things, and we don't want to argue anymore. But you aren't responsible for any part of that, and it doesn't change how much we love you.

Am I going to have to change schools?
Say: I hope not, but we don't have all the decisions made yet. If there is anything we can do to keep you in the same house/neighborhood/school, we will try our best to make that happen. We both love you and want to do what's best for our family.

Are you going to get back together?
Say: I'm sorry. This is a hard decision for us, but we aren't going to be married anymore. We both love you, but the two of us need to be able to find our own happiness.

Why is Mom/Dad moving out?
Say: Your mom/dad and I have some big problems that we can't work out. We aren't going to be married and live together anymore. But we will both still love you and care for you just the same when you spend time with each of us.

PART
TWO

DURING DIVORCE PROCEEDINGS

Now that your divorce is underway, you're going to need new information, new tools, and renewed strength to protect yourself and your children from the conflict and the crazy. This part of your journey can be the longest and most difficult.

First, we'll talk about how the extra stress may be impacting you. Chapter 4 will explain some of the common reactions to high-conflict divorce and recommend some coping strategies to help you feel more in control and make better decisions.

Chapter 5 is all about the legal process. Being familiar with and prepared for the legal process will help you avoid common high-conflict divorce mistakes. We'll explore how property is divided and discuss child support, custody, and spousal support. Next, you'll learn about the steps in the divorce process, what to expect from your spouse, and how to keep your cool.

Finally, chapter 6 is all about keeping your children protected and safe during a high-conflict divorce. Custody battles, hostile communication, and co-parenting challenges can make it difficult to stay on the high road. This chapter offers tips for trying to make co-parenting work, communicating safely and effectively, resolving parenting plan issues, and addressing safety concerns so you can support your children in the best possible way.

CHAPTER FOUR

THE EMOTIONAL IMPACT

High-conflict divorce is not your normal everyday kind of stress. Overbooking your schedule, running late for a meeting, getting called into your boss' office, or getting a flat tire—those might make you feel stressed and overwhelmed, temporarily. But high-conflict divorce can be so traumatic and enduring that it impacts both your brain and your body.

Understanding the reactions you might have, knowing what to look out for, and learning new ways to cope with the emotional rollercoaster of high-conflict divorce can keep you on a healthy and productive path. Let's explore.

WHAT YOU MIGHT BE FEELING

Divorce is hard on everyone. Breaking up a family, dividing up property, and navigating a "new normal" are difficult tasks, even when the split is amicable. When you're divorcing a high-conflict personality, the word "stress" may not even begin to describe what you're feeling.

Chronic Stress and Trauma

Normal stress can be a good thing. It urges us to protect ourselves and take action. Our bodies are designed to respond to stress. At the first sign of danger, they automatically release stress hormones in preparation for fight or flight. Our muscles tense, breathing quickens, heart rate increases, and digestive processes slow down to provide energy to other areas so we can be ready to fight for survival.

Once the danger has passed, our stress hormone levels return to normal. Muscles relax, breathing slows down and deepens, and our heart goes back to its normal, steady rhythm.

But when we're faced with chronic, lasting stress, those hormone levels stay elevated. Our bodies aren't designed for that. Over time, this imbalance can take a toll on both emotional and physical health.

If we are living in a toxic relationship or going through a high-conflict divorce, our bodies may be programmed to stay in this state of alarm, where we're constantly on alert.

You may be fighting to stay in your home, keep custody of your children, or even stay out of jail or rehab. Conflict, dirty divorce tricks, and constant fear can justifiably cause you to experience very real trauma.

As you read through some of the emotional reactions that follow, pay attention to which ones you've been experiencing and to what degree they've been affecting your life. You may want to start documenting these so you can track if symptoms are improving or getting worse over time. Often, we're so distracted by keeping up with the daily grind that we don't notice changes in our own mental and physical health until something drastic happens.

Common Reactions

Everyone reacts differently when faced with a life crisis. Your individual response can depend on a number of factors, including your personality, health, childhood, prior adult events, experience in your marriage or other relationships, and the level of conflict in your divorce.

You may be experiencing:

Being overwhelmed: Feeling like you can't handle things, procrastinating, avoiding

Fatigue or tiredness: Feeling sluggish and worn down, the kind of tired that a good night's rest doesn't alleviate

Sadness or depression: Extended bouts of crying, not wanting to be social, lack of interest, trouble concentrating

Fear, anxiety, or panic attacks: Feeling more afraid than usual, being easily startled, feeling jumpy, or worrying excessively

Anger or irritability: Difficulty managing anger, feeling irritated by minor things, easily frustrated, complaining more than usual

Obsessing or ruminating: Getting stuck in negative thoughts, thinking about the same things over and over

Guilt, self-blame: Self-criticism, feelings of shame, feeling responsible, not good enough

Changes in weight or appetite: Eating more or less than usual, sudden weight loss or gain, lack of appetite

Headaches or migraines: Experiencing headaches or migraines more frequently, with greater severity, or of longer duration

Difficulty sleeping or nightmares: Insomnia, inability to stay asleep, waking early, nightmares or night terrors

Muscle tension: Tightness in neck or shoulders, leg cramps, stiffness, clenching your jaw

Heartburn, nausea, or vomiting: Difficulty eating or keeping down food, feeling nauseated, burning sensation in throat or chest

Change in bowel habits: Constipation or diarrhea, IBS

Changes in menstrual cycle: Longer or more painful periods, less frequent or skipped periods

Body aches: General complaints of pain

All of these symptoms are normal. Most everyone going through divorce experiences some of these at one time or another.

But depending on your personal history and the amount of conflict you're experiencing, you may find that you're really struggling. Take care to monitor your own bodily responses and the impact they may be having on your life. Ask a friend or your counselor to keep an eye out for any changes they notice.

When to Get Professional Help

See your doctor or a mental health professional if symptoms are upsetting you or impacting your ability to perform daily activities, work, or care for your children or parents. The sooner you seek help, the easier it will be to address the symptoms. Keep documentation that you are getting assistance—this documentation can help protect you if needed.

According to the American Psychiatric Association, below are more serious conditions to watch for.

Depression

Depression is a common condition that can affect your ability to enjoy life. Some people continue to function with depression even though they feel quite low. Others may find it difficult to work or get out of bed. Depression is serious but also very treatable with therapy, coping tools, and/or medication. If left untreated, it can create a downward spiral and an inability to see a way out.

If you are having thoughts of hurting yourself, please get help immediately. Call 911 or the National Suicide Prevention Lifeline at 1-800-273-TALK (8255).

Symptoms can vary from mild to severe and can include:

- Sadness or depressed mood
- Decreased interest or pleasure in activities you once enjoyed
- Changes in appetite or weight

- Difficulty sleeping or sleeping too much
- Fatigue or loss of energy
- Agitation or restlessness, or slowed movements and speech (observable by others)
- Feelings of worthlessness or guilt
- Difficulty thinking, concentrating, or making decisions
- Thoughts of death or suicide

Anxiety

Many people experience anxiety from time to time. But if you are spending a significant amount of your day worrying when there is no real threat, or your worry is out of proportion to the situation, it can affect other parts of your life. Psychotherapy, self-help, and medications can be very effective in helping you manage your anxiety.

Symptoms of general anxiety may include:

- Excessive anxiety or worry about a variety of things
- Worry that is difficult to control
- Restlessness
- Feeling keyed up or on edge
- Fatigue
- Difficulty concentrating or mind going blank
- Irritability
- Muscle tension
- Difficulty falling or staying asleep, or restless, unsatisfying sleep
- Sweating, nausea, or diarrhea

It's normal to feel really stressed, anxious, or sad when exposed to a traumatic event. Many people recover, but some continue to experience difficult symptoms and memories related to the event. Personal history, genetics, social support, and many other factors can affect whether someone might develop PTSD from a traumatic experience. Psychotherapy, medication, and other alternatives are used in treatment.

PTSD symptoms may look like:

Intrusive memories: recurrent, distressing memories or nightmares; reliving the traumatic event as if it were happening again (flashbacks); severe emotional distress or physical reactions to something that reminds you of the traumatic event

Avoidance: trying to avoid thinking or talking about the traumatic event; avoiding places, activities, or people that remind you of the traumatic event

Negative changes in thinking and mood: negative thoughts about yourself, other people, or the world; hopelessness about the future; memory problems; difficulty maintaining close relationships; lack of interest in activities you once enjoyed; feeling emotionally numb

Changes in physical and emotional reactions: being easily startled or frightened; self-destructive behavior; difficulty sleeping or concentrating; irritability, angry outbursts, or aggressive behavior; overwhelming guilt or shame

Why Managing Your Emotions Matters

Big feelings are part of high-conflict divorce, and finding safe people to share those with is essential. There are three very important reasons to pay close attention to any reactions you're having and find ways to manage and cope appropriately:

1. **You can't make good decisions when your nervous system is dysregulated.**

Divorce is all about decisions. What to say, what to do, how to negotiate, when to settle, when to stick to your guns. It's not a good option to ignore what's happening nor to lash out in anger. Neither will get you what you want or what's best for your future or your children.

2. **Failure to manage your emotional state could be used against you.**

If you are failing to function well as a result of your emotional reactions, your spouse could be documenting it. Explosive texts or social media posts could be used to portray *you* as the high-conflict person. Something as simple as the kids mentioning that mom was too tired to make dinner last night can become fuel for their custody arguments.

3. **Other people are affected when you don't manage your emotions.**

When you aren't coping well, your children, co-workers, friends, and family also take the hit. As hard as this is on you, your children need to be able to rely on you as a parent who provides stability and comfort, not someone who adds to their burden. Your employer still has to be able to count on you to show up and do your job effectively. Family and friends don't deserve to be targets of your anger or have to tiptoe around your anxieties.

Your emotional health is so important. Staying emotionally balanced will enable you to survive the divorce, support your children, and create your best future. Please don't ignore what you're feeling and how it's affecting you. You may not be able to change your situation, but you can put measures and practices in place to help you live better while you're going through it.

WAYS TO COPE

Many well-researched self-help practices, therapies, and treatments exist to help you manage any reactions or symptoms you may be experiencing. Keeping your emotional system regulated will benefit you in myriad ways.

Try as many of the following suggestions as you like. Experiment to see what works for you. Stick with it until you find the combination that keeps you feeling more centered and in control.

Mental and Spiritual Practices

Journaling

Writing down your thoughts and feelings can be a powerful tool to help you to process your emotions. Science has shown that simply naming what you're feeling can lessen its impact. Once you name that feeling, you have much more control over it.

Journaling methods range from free-writing in a journal to online apps. Jot a single sentence, write bullet points, draw a picture, or write a novel. Do an online search for journaling prompts if you need guidance.

Here are a few to get you started:

- How am I feeling today?
- What sensations am I feeling in my body?
- What negative thoughts am I repeating to myself today, and what's the reality?
- What do I need today to care for myself?
- What am I afraid of?
- What do I need to let go of?
- Am I trying to control something that's not mine to control?
- Did I ask for help when I needed it?
- Do I need to make a change in my habits?
- What coping skills did I use to handle challenges today?
- What did I do that I was proud of today?
- What can I do to make tomorrow better?
- What am I learning about myself?

Meditation

You don't need to be a Buddhist monk to begin a meditation practice. You don't even need a yoga mat. All you need is a few minutes, a quiet space, and a bit of mindfulness.

Meditation creates a deep sense of mind-body well-being that can promote feelings of balance and peace. While there are many forms of meditation practices, they all share elements of focused attention and relaxed breathing.

The proven benefits of meditation include:

- Increased self-awareness
- Reduced stress
- Reduced anxiety
- Reduced depression
- Improved ability to regulate emotions
- Increased patience and tolerance
- Increased memory
- Increased focus and attention
- Increased immune response
- Decreased pain

There are many types of meditation to choose from, including mindfulness, guided meditation, qigong, Tai chi, transcendental meditation, and more. Mindful meditation is free and can be done with no equipment. Here are a few tips on how you might start with that practice:

Step 1: Choose a time and place.

> Experts tell us that we have the best chance of success if we create a routine and stick to it.

Step 2: Decide how long you'll spend.

> Start with a short time period—even three minutes. As you strengthen your meditation muscles, you can build up your time and find what feels right for you.

Step 3: Sit comfortably.

> Sit in a chair with your feet on the floor or on the floor with your legs crossed. Align your posture so that your back is straight, but not tensed.

> Close your eyes, breathe slowly, and check in with your
> body to notice any places that feel tense or tight. Now bring
> your attention to your thoughts. Acknowledge them and let
> them pass without judgment. If your mind wanders, gently
> bring your attention back to your breath and your thoughts.

See Resources (page 185) for more information.

Gratitude Lists

Science has shown that those who practice gratitude enjoy
better physical and emotional health and are happier and more
satisfied with life. They also experience less depression, and
are more resilient following traumatic events.

You can increase your own capacity for gratitude by taking
time to create daily gratitude lists. Simply write down three
things each day that you are grateful for. Studies show that you
will notice an improvement by doing this for just 21 days.

Counter Negative Thinking

Our own internal dialogue can add to feelings of anxiety and
stress. Human brains are programmed to focus on the negative in order to remember and protect us from those things in
the future. But that also creates stronger connections in the
brain, which can make negative thoughts attract even more
negative thoughts.

The first key to overcoming negative thinking is aware-
ness. If you can be present with those negative thoughts and
acknowledge them, then you have the opportunity to examine
them and perhaps change them. Remember, you don't have
to believe everything you think. It might be time to let go of

those thought patterns and self-limiting beliefs that have been holding you back.

See **What to Say When** (page 88) for more tips.

Cultivate Social Connections

Humans are not designed to live in isolation. We are wired for connection and closeness. If your tendency is to crawl off into a corner when you're stressed, or if you've been putting others first and letting your own social network dwindle, then this is a great time to step back out into the world.

It's not always easy to make new friends as an adult—just remember that there are people just like you out there also looking for support and connection. You can try the following:

- Reconnect with old friends
- Look for a group that focuses on your area of interest
- Join an exercise class, book club, or spiritual/religious study group
- Invite a colleague, classmate, or neighbor for coffee
- Take your dog to the dog park
- Volunteer
- Take adult classes at the local college

Take Up a New Hobby

This is a great time to start learning something you've always wanted to do. Take up scrapbooking, knitting, woodworking, upholstery, hiking, cycling, antiquing, painting, sculpting, or anything your heart desires.

Learning and engaging in a fun activity will stimulate your brain, keep your mind off your troubles, and build confidence.

If you join a group or a class, you'll also be building new social connections, and it might even open your eyes to a new career.

Physical Practices

Yoga

Like meditation, yoga has long been respected as a practice to promote both emotional and physical well-being. It also provides increased flexibility and mobility, improved strength, and pain relief.

Styles of yoga vary from restful and meditative to active and strenuous. Look for classes near you or find free videos online to get started (see Resources, page 185). If you're new to the practice of yoga, be gentle with yourself as you learn the language and the poses. Alignment is important, so use props or follow the modified poses until you can achieve the full pose in correct position.

You might also search for a certified yoga therapist who works in a holistic manner with the whole body and mind. Yoga therapy can help with anxiety, depression, PTSD, insomnia, pain, and more.

Exercise

The benefits of exercise for reducing stress, anxiety, and depression are well documented and far-reaching. Regular exercise can reduce the levels of stress hormones like adrenaline and increase the levels of feel-good hormones like serotonin and dopamine.

Exercise has also been shown to affect the brain, specifically the hippocampus, which is involved in learning, memory, and regulating emotions. By increasing blood supply, and thus oxygen and nutrients, to the brain, exercise stimulates the building of new neurons. Scientists believe this process creates the opportunity for us to acquire new information, see new solutions, and adapt to change.

So how much exercise is enough to make a difference?

I will start by saying every minute counts. But to make a real impact, the Centers for Disease Control and Prevention recommend that adults get at least 150 to 300 minutes a week of moderate-intensity aerobic activity (anything that gets your heart beating faster). Just walking briskly for 30 minutes, five days a week, is enough to boost your mood, improve sleep, and reduce anxiety.

Outdoor exercise may give you an extra boost. Numerous studies show that vitamin D, which is produced by our bodies when we're exposed to sunlight, can help prevent depression and lift our mood. Light therapy that mimics outdoor light can also be effective. Consult with your doctor to determine the best light for you.

Massage

Massage isn't just for pampering; it has real health benefits. Therapeutic and medical massage is now commonly accepted as a viable practice for lowering stress, lifting mood, improving sleep, reducing pain, and relieving a variety of conditions. It can also provide a source of care, touch, and connection that separated and divorcing people can be missing.

Check your local area for licensed massage therapists, who can provide a variety of related services. It's important to communicate with your therapist. Complete the intake form fully, ask questions, undress to the level of your comfort, and let them know if the level of pressure is too light or too hard, if there are areas you would like them to concentrate on, or if anything is making you uncomfortable.

Massage may be covered by your insurance if your doctor recommends it for a medical condition, or if it's part of your chiropractic care plan.

Wellness Checks

You rely on your body 24/7 to take care of you. Regular doctor and dentist visits will make sure that everything is running at peak performance. If something isn't just right, small adjustments can head off bigger problems later.

Start with your primary care provider. They can check your vitals, run blood work, and refer you to other specialists if needed. If your partner was unfaithful, please get an STD check right away. Your family doctor can also help you address any troubling symptoms like insomnia, depression, or anxiety.

Next, is it time to visit your gynecologist, eye doctor, or dentist? Get those appointments on the calendar. Eye strain or tooth pain can cause headaches and other problems. Menopausal symptoms or changes in your menstrual cycle should be evaluated.

Schedule your mammogram, colonoscopy, or any other procedures you're due for. You'll feel better knowing that all is well, and if you have children, you'll be modeling great self-care to them.

Healthy Diet

When life gets stressful, sometimes eating well falls off the priority list. You might be skipping meals or turning to junk or convenience foods. But mounting evidence suggests that a diet high in carbohydrates, fat, and processed sugars might make us feel worse than we already do. In other words, there is a direct correlation between mood and food.

Nutritional psychiatrists at Harvard compare our brain to a luxury car, and suggest that we operate best when we feed our brains premium fuel. Try a diet free of processed foods and sugar for two to three weeks, focusing instead on lean proteins, vegetables, and whole grains. You might also try adding in fermented foods like kombucha. These changes may have a tremendous impact on how you feel.

A food diary may help you pinpoint those foods that help your mood and any that cause trouble.

Vitamins and Supplements

In my experience, people have reported feeling better when they have tried:

- Daily multivitamin
- Probiotics
- B vitamins
- Vitamin D
- Magnesium
- Omega-3
- St. John's Wort

If your diet has been less than optimal or you've been getting less exercise and outdoor time than recommended, supplements may help bring your vitamin levels back up until you can develop your new habits.

Check with your physician before taking any supplement to ensure that it is right for you and doesn't interfere with any of your other medications.

Psychotherapy and Related Treatments

If your symptoms are severe or the methods discussed haven't been successful, therapy and related treatments may be right for you. Let's explore some options.

One-on-One Therapy

One-on-one meetings with a counselor can allow you to explore what you're feeling and find solutions to self-limiting beliefs or behaviors. Talking with someone who can validate you and offer another perspective may help you feel less alone, increase your self-awareness, and give you more strength and confidence. Many therapists offer phone or video sessions, so don't let location deter you.

If you suspect you are experiencing trauma symptoms, seek out a therapist who specializes in treating trauma victims and PTSD.

Support Groups

As mentioned earlier, support groups can be a wonderful source of support, friendship, validation, and shared experiences. Counselor-led and volunteer-led support groups are available both in person and online.

Not all support groups are created equal, so check them out. A group of people complaining or venting about all the bad things in their lives will not be helpful to you. Look for groups that are therapeutic in nature, focused on healing and recovery.

Check with local hospitals, churches, and counseling centers for suggestions.

Complementary Therapies

In addition to traditional talk therapy, some new modalities are being used with success, especially with trauma victims.

Somatic Therapy

Somatic therapy is a body-centered approach based on the idea that the body holds on to past traumas, which disrupts the nervous system. This method uses both psychotherapy and physical therapies to free the body from the past and release tension.

Somatic therapy sessions may include talk therapy, meditation, dance, breathing techniques, voice work, physical exercise, movement, and massage.

Look for a licensed professional counselor with advanced training in somatic therapy.

Tapping

Emotional freedom technique, or tapping, is an alternative treatment that stimulates the body's energy points—the same ones that are focused on in acupuncture and acupressure—by tapping them with your fingertips.

Researchers at Harvard Medical School discovered that stimulating these points lessened stress and fear in the amygdala—the part of our brain that alerts us to threats or danger. Further studies reported drastic reductions in PTSD symptoms and stress hormones.

See Resources (page 185) for more information.

Eye Movement Desensitization and Reprocessing (EMDR)

EMDR is a psychotherapy treatment that can accelerate healing from psychological trauma. The therapist uses bilateral stimulation, which may include eye movements, taps, or tones while the client focuses on a target memory.

EMDR therapy is recognized by the American Psychiatric Association, the World Health Organization, and the Department of Defense as an effective treatment for trauma. Numerous studies have shown significant reduction or even elimination of PTSD symptoms after three to 12 sessions.

WHAT TO SAY WHEN

During high-conflict divorce, you might find yourself getting stuck in what's sometimes called "stinking thinking":

- This is so unfair.
- My kids are going to hate me/be messed up forever.
- No one cares what I've been through.
- I'll never see my kids/pay my bills/feel okay again.
- I feel helpless/I'm not strong enough.

Yes, this may be one of the toughest times you'll ever endure. But according to the American Psychological Association, ruminating on negative thoughts can fuel depression, impair thinking and problem-solving, and drive away critical social support. So, what can you do to break the cycle when you find yourself stuck?

Try repeating a mantra or a positive phrase to counter that negative thought:

- I can still make the best possible choices for myself.
- I'm a great parent and I can love my children through this.
- I do have people who love and care about me.
- I will have what I need in my life—maybe not right now, but soon.
- I can do hard things. I've made it this far and I can keep going.

Use self-talk to challenge negative thoughts. Ask yourself questions like:

- Is this a feeling or a fact?
- Is this helpful?
- Will this help me get what I want?
- Is this an inconvenience or a tragedy?
- Is there another way to look at this?

CHAPTER FIVE

NAVIGATING THE COURTS

Unless you're an attorney or a paralegal, the divorce process and court system can seem like a foreign language. And if you haven't had much experience with the family law system before, you might be surprised to learn this hard truth: The judge is not interested in how hurt or angry you are or how unfair things are—he/she cares what the law says.

There is no emotional justice in a court of law, only facts. Your best chance of getting the settlement or award that you want is to understand what the law says and present the best evidence to support your request in a businesslike manner.

In this chapter, we'll review some basics of property distribution, child custody, child support, and spousal support. Then we'll get you ready for the legal process by reviewing the steps and phases, predicting your partner's behavior, and exploring how to handle yourself in mediation or court.

Just like all other aspects of high-conflict divorce, preparation and knowing what to expect are your best chance to have a good, safe outcome.

Please note, information contained here is not intended to replace legal counsel. Consult with a lawyer for advice on your particular issue or case.

UNDERSTANDING DISTRIBUTION OF PROPERTY

This literally means dividing up everything you own as a married couple, including assets like your home, business, bank accounts, and retirement funds, as well as debts such as a mortgage, car loans, and credit card debt. It also includes all your "stuff," from the dishes to the lawnmower. Everything considered to be marital property will be divided in your divorce, but your separate property is yours to keep.

Three key concepts impact how that property gets divided:

- Community property vs. equitable distribution
- Marital property vs. separate property
- Marital misconduct

Separate Property

Property that is clearly yours and not acquired with marital income or assets remains with you and is not up for division. These items are generally considered separate property:

- Property owned by one spouse before the marriage
- Gifts given to and intended for one spouse
- Inheritances received before or during the marriage
- Some personal injury awards

Commingling separate property with marital property can be tricky. If you received an inheritance and used it to pay for part of your marital home, you may have forfeited your right to claim that money as separate property unless you can provide clear documentation tracing the source of those funds.

Community Property

States that follow "community property" rules treat all earnings, property, and debt acquired during the marriage as owned by both spouses equally. At divorce (or separation), that property will be divided 50/50. Community property states are Louisiana, Arizona, California, Texas, Washington, Idaho, Nevada, New Mexico, and Wisconsin.

Equitable Distribution

All states not listed in the previous section are considered "equitable distribution" states. Under these rules, property will be divided on an "equitable or fair" basis. The standard or most common split is still 50/50; however, judges have authority to award a larger portion of the marital estate to one spouse based on a number of factors. Each state's statutes vary slightly, but here are some common considerations:

- Education, earning capacity, age, and health of each spouse
- Marital standard of living
- Spouse's separate assets and sources of income
- Effect of tax liabilities
- Future financial needs and liabilities of each spouse
- Premarital agreements
- Support obligations from a prior marriage
- Any other factor deemed by the court to be just and proper

Financial Misconduct

Most state laws allow for a redistribution of assets in the case of financial misconduct or dissipation of marital assets. According to the Ohio Bar Association:

"If there has been financial misconduct, the court may divide the assets unequally, in order to appropriately compensate the harmed spouse."

This misconduct is generally defined as significant gambling losses, failure to disclose an asset in earlier proceedings, money spent on an extramarital affair, or the purchase of illegal substances. The harmed spouse must be prepared to provide proof.

Final Property Distribution Cautions

Property distribution is typically not modifiable once your divorce is finalized and filed with the courts. It is vital that you understand up front what you are agreeing to and that you are willing to live with it.

Be sure you understand not only what you are legally entitled to, but the short-term, long-term, and tax implications of certain property divisions.

If you are considering keeping the marital home, be sure to also consider all the costs of upkeep, cash required for emergency repairs, and the assets that you may need to give up to offset your partner's share of the equity in the home.

Let's look at a common example. Your partner proposes they take $10,000 from the checking account and you take $10,000 from the retirement account. This may look like an even settlement, but you will pay tax on your $10,000 when you withdraw it and may pay a 10 percent early withdrawal penalty if you are under 59½ years old. So, you might receive $7,000 to their $10,000, which is definitely not an equitable distribution.

If arguing your case to a judge for a specific division of assets, be prepared to show evidence why that particular distribution is equitable. If necessary, hire a financial professional to act as an expert witness.

UNDERSTANDING CHILD CUSTODY

The idea of losing any time with the children strikes fear in the hearts of most parents. Experts agree that children do best when they spend generous amounts of time with both parents, and the courts are generally supportive of this notion.

Coming to agreement on child custody and visitation is often one of the most contentious issues in high-conflict divorce. Your spouse may be fighting to the death for more than the standard shared parenting plan or even seeking sole custody for a few reasons:

* More time with children means less child support (see Understanding Child Support, page 98).
* It's an opportunity to kick you where it hurts most.
* They will have decision-making control.

First, let's review some important concepts about custody.

Legal Custody

Legal custody refers only to decision-making authority. This determines who will have the ability to make decisions regarding the children in areas such as education, non-emergency medical care, and religious upbringing.

Legal custody can be either "sole," in which only one parent has this authority, or "joint," in which both (or either) parents can make these decisions. It's important to understand that parents can have "joint legal custody" without sharing physical custody.

Joint legal custody can be a challenge in high-conflict situations, since the acrimonious relationship makes any collaborative decision making nearly impossible. Be certain you specify exactly how joint decisions will be made.

Physical Custody

Physical custody, also known as "residential custody," determines where the child lives most of the time. Just like with legal custody, there are several ways physical custody can be defined in your agreement. One parent is designated as the residential parent for purposes of school enrollment. Possibilities include:

Sole: The child lives primarily with one parent, and the other parent is granted certain visitation rights, such as a weekday or two and weekend overnights at the other parent's home.

Joint/Shared: The child spends a relatively equal amount of time at each parent's home. In many states, this is the prevailing standard.

Bird Nest: In this scenario, the children remain in one home (usually the marital home), and the parents, who each have their own separate residences, move in and out according to their parenting schedule.

Visitation

Unsupervised: The most common scenario, this allows either parent to take the children to their home, to events, to school, on outings, and generally be unrestricted. Some parenting plans may include provisions that the other parent be notified or give permission if the parent wants to take the child out of state or out of the country.

Supervised: This may be used in cases where sexual abuse, physical abuse, addiction, mental illness, anger, or other issues make it potentially unsafe for the child to be alone with that parent. The visitation must occur in the presence of another responsible adult or a representative of the court at a specified location.

Virtual: Video chat apps provide the opportunity for children and parents who are separated by distance to connect on a regular basis.

When it comes to custody matters, your spouse may pull some really evil tricks. Recall the mother in chapter 2 who lost custody and was sent to rehab because she napped on the couch and her spouse fabricated a story?

This low-life behavior isn't typical, but it does happen. That's why it's so important to take the high road, shut down social media, and essentially live like a camera is following you around while your divorce is pending. Your partner may be looking for anything that could be twisted in their favor.

Child Custody Considerations

Most states have some version of a parenting plan that outlines your agreement on legal custody, physical custody, visitation, medical insurance, expenses, education, extracurricular activities, and more.

I recommend in any high-conflict divorce that you also ask the court (or your spouse) to utilize a co-parenting app or software to communicate, schedule, and share expenses (see Resources on page 185). It can take much of the stress out of the co-parenting relationship and provides a record for the court of any high-conflict behavior or failure to meet obligations. Some of the full-service co-parenting apps cost 80 to 100 dollars per year, but they can be good investments since they include many features to keep you organized and protected.

UNDERSTANDING CHILD SUPPORT

Each state has its own child support laws that provide for distribution of income to ensure that children are supported by both parents. All states have a formula to calculate these payments, and although other factors are considered, generally speaking, child support contributions are often proportional to each parent's respective incomes.

Child support is intended to cover basic living expenses for the children. Most parenting plans include additional language to outline sharing of expenses for extras like school tuition, fees, and extracurricular activities.

Basic child support calculations are based on income from all sources, and the primary factors that influence the amount of child support are:

- Number of children
- Total family income
- Custody/parenting time
- Medical insurance coverage

Ask that any child support payments be paid to you through your local child support enforcement agency. That will offer protection should payments fall behind.

The dirty divorce tricks that your spouse may try to pull include fighting for additional parenting time and voluntarily being unemployed or underemployed.

Be prepared to prove that income should be imputed to your spouse. This means to assign an income to them based on what they should be able to earn, not what they are earning now.

For instance, if your spouse had been working as an engineer earning $100,000 a year and suddenly decides to become a part-time barista making $12,000, the court is going to see right through that and will likely assign them a much higher income for the basis of child support calculations.

UNDERSTANDING ALIMONY (SPOUSAL SUPPORT)

Long gone are the days when spousal support was a given and it was permanent or lasted for decades. Most spousal support (also called maintenance or alimony) these days is intended to be rehabilitative, meaning it will support you until you are able to support yourself. The court generally expects you to get whatever training or education is necessary and then go back to work.

Unlike child support, only a few states have a calculation for spousal support. It is often left to the sole discretion of the judge to decide how spousal support will be determined. An attorney who practices frequently in your local court will know how the judge assigned to your case typically handles spousal support. They can give you a range and a fairly good idea of how the judge would rule, which is good information to know when it comes to negotiation.

A day in court plus all the prep time could cost you $5,000 to $10,000 or more in lawyer fees. You don't want to waste time and money going to court requesting an amount that you don't have a chance of getting. On the other hand, if your spouse offers you $1,000 a month for three years, and you know the judge is likely to award you $2,000 a month for five years, that's an $84,000 difference and may be worth the cost of going to court.

Types of Spousal Support

Temporary: Paid to the recipient spouse while the divorce action is pending.

Rehabilitative: Paid for a certain number of years until the recipient can get training to become self-sufficient or complete raising the children.

Permanent: Final award amount once the divorce is finalized. Permanent spousal support can be awarded for any length of time. Typically, this is based on the length of the marriage (a longer marriage would result in longer support) and is the monthly payment model you may be most familiar with.

Lump Sum: Rather than an ongoing monthly payment, the recipient spouse receives one large payment at a specified time.

Factors Considered

When determining the amount and duration of spousal support, the following general factors are taken into account:

- Recipient spouse's need
- Length of the marriage
- Payor spouse's ability to pay
- Number and ages of children
- Previous marital lifestyle
- Age and health of both spouses
- Fault

Let's look at some examples:

You have been married 35 years, have adult children, are 60 years old, your spouse makes $150,000, and you make $10,000. You may have a good argument for spousal support. Your marriage is long term and your ability to retrain and reenter the job market at 60 may not provide you with income earning opportunities to support yourself.

You have been married five years, have a three-year-old, are 30 years old, your spouse makes $50,000 and you make $45,000. That might be a more difficult argument. Your marriage is of shorter duration, your incomes are relatively equivalent, and you have time to increase your earning capacity.

Adjustment or Termination

Spousal support can be modified when circumstances change. That means that you or your ex can return to the court to have spousal support adjusted either up or down. You may have the option to make it non-modifiable, but weigh those risks and benefits with your attorney. Non-modifiable protects you from your ex reducing their income but leaves you vulnerable in the event that you become ill or unable to work.

Laws vary by state, but it is common for spousal support to terminate upon death of either the payor or recipient, or upon remarriage or cohabitation by the recipient.

So be aware. Moving in right away with your new "friend" may terminate your right to spousal support.

WHAT TO EXPECT WHEN YOU GET TO COURT

The legal process of getting divorced includes many steps before you get to court to have a judge decide your case. Most (95 percent) of all divorces settle before this point, sometimes in the hallway right before trial. That being said, some high-conflict spouses won't be satisfied to negotiate any kind of agreement and want their day in court.

Being Prepared for Harsh Realities

Going to court so that a judge can hear your side and understand how crazy your partner is may sound like a great idea. But in reality, you must be prepared that:

* High-conflict people can be charming and persuasive.
* Abuse or addiction allegations against you may initially be believed.
* Officials may assume you are both equally at fault for the conflict.
* Your spouse may not be held accountable for perjury or contempt.
* Your reality and definition of fair isn't what matters, nor will a judge want to hear it.
* The time to present your argument is very limited.

BUT THAT ISN'T FAIR!

I know, and I wish I could tell you something different, but I can't. Just because you have truth on your side or have a strong argument doesn't mean the judge will see it or rule that way.

That's one reason I recommend you find a mediator who is skilled in handling high-conflict cases. There will be much more opportunity for the mediator to see your spouse's true character and intervene with conflict resolution strategies. There is a possibility of de-escalating things, which will save you money and get your divorce finalized more quickly. In mediation, you have more control over the pace and the decisions (see page 43).

Hearings

Before your divorce is finalized, you may have a number of hearings.

Hearings are primarily held to schedule the remainder of your divorce proceedings and to issue any temporary orders that need to be in place until the divorce is finalized. These might include:

- Temporary child support, spousal support, custody, and visitation
- Payment of a spouse's legal fees
- Determination of who lives in the marital home, and who pays the mortgage/rent and repairs
- Financial restraining orders
- Protection or no-contact orders
- Orders to comply with discovery requests
- Anything needed to stabilize the situation and/or move your case forward through the divorce process

The attorneys, magistrates, and judge may have conversations alone, or the hearings may be held in a courtroom. Typically, your attorney will do most of the talking. If you are asked to testify, be calm, professional, and businesslike. Answer truthfully, briefly, to the point, and do not argue with either your spouse's attorney or the judge. See **What to Say When** (page 112) for more pointers.

Trial

Prior to appearing in court for an actual divorce trial, you may have gone through a lengthy discovery, investigative, and negotiation process, including:

- Financial disclosures
- Interrogatories and requests for documents
- Depositions
- Interviews with psychologists, vocational experts, a guardian ad litem, social workers, and more
- Mediation
- Parenting classes
- Attorney-to-attorney negotiation
- Hearings
- Settlement conferences

When the day of the trial comes, you can expect to feel nervous even if you are well prepared and have a strong case. The courtroom might feel formal, the procedures will be new to you, and there is no guarantee how the judge will rule. But at the end of the day or days, you will finally be done—all that's left is to wait for the judge's final ruling and the divorce will be finalized. The judge may not rule while you are in court, so be prepared to wait weeks until the final ruling is filed.

Your attorney will review your case with you and prepare you for any testifying you may be asked to do. You may even run through some practice sessions to make sure you feel comfortable and understand how to respond to different types of questions.

PREDICTING YOUR SPOUSE'S BEHAVIOR

As you might expect, the high-conflict person isn't likely to cooperate, play fair, or follow the rules. The tactics they employ may range from frustrating to downright dirty. Here are a few things that might happen:

Delays and Omissions

Hearings, mediation, and conferences will be continually rescheduled at the last minute because of their "unavailability" or "illness." Your partner will let a deadline pass without acting at all or by omitting things. If you ask for three years of checking account statements within 15 days, it may require several follow-ups by your attorney to get that request fulfilled. Then, there may be months missing. Review everything carefully.

Allegations of Abuse/Addiction

Your partner may try to portray you as an alcoholic or pain pill addict, mentally ill, or abusive either to them or your children. If you have any reason to believe they might pull this move, notify your attorney immediately and follow their advice. Begin documenting your partner's behavior as well as your own.

Your behavior must be squeaky clean. Either go no-contact or use the communication method from chapter 1 (page 10).

No partying, no dating. Take the high road when it comes to the children. The court may initially be influenced by your spouse's emotional appeal, but your statements of fact and your documented actions are your defense.

Reducing/Hiding Income

As soon as they get an idea that divorce is in their future, high-conflict people may begin minimizing their income in order to pay less spousal support or child support. You'll know this trick is being played if your spouse who made $80,000 a year is now claiming they make $40,000. Two ways to address this are imputing income and lifestyle analysis.

Imputing income means asking the court to assign the income that your spouse should be making based on their income history and skills. Lifestyle analysis would include looking at their expenses and spending to prove that $40,000 couldn't possibly support their current lifestyle and that there must be a hidden source of income somewhere.

You will need documentation to prove that your spouse has hidden assets not reported on their financial disclosure, or that they moved money from joint accounts prior to or during the divorce action.

Parental Alienation

If you have children, this is one of the dirtiest plays in the high-conflict handbook. Your spouse will try to recruit your own children to their team of haters. By blaming you, telling lies, and even using other friends and family members, they make every attempt to get the child to side with them to such an extent that the child doesn't want to spend time with you.

They want custody of the children in order to have a win, to pay less child support, and because it will hurt you. Again, squeaky-clean behavior should be your strategy. You want to be the one attempting to co-parent amicably, supporting your children in loving their other parent, and keeping conflict and criticism out of your kids' world.

Meet the Girlfriend/Enemy

What better way to rattle you than to show up everywhere with the new love interest in tow? Or worse yet, they may have recruited your own siblings or parents against you. Take a deep breath, tell yourself how grateful you are that you will soon be divorced from this person, and then put on your game face. Regulating your emotions is the way to win against a high-conflict person. They take pleasure in seeing you upset and hope that you won't present yourself in the best possible manner.

Contempt/Failure to Comply

During and after divorce, it's common for high-conflict personalities to choose not to follow court orders. They might fail to keep your parenting schedule, cancel insurance, change beneficiaries, or refuse to pay spousal support, child support, or other bills that have been ordered.

Extraneous Motions

Taking you back to court is a favorite activity for some high-conflict people. They love to file motions for anything they can think of—whether you failed to copy them on a school schedule, you were late for parenting time, or they think you aren't giving the children enough vegetables.

HOW TO HANDLE YOURSELF IN MEDIATION OR COURT

All humans have biases, including judges, and you are more likely to gain their support if they like and respect you.

Conduct yourself in such a way that you are:

* Respectful of the process and the court
* Seen as a viable, credible witness
* Heard and believed
* Honest and forthcoming
* Trying to be cooperative
* Putting your children's best interests first
* Being more than fair in what you are requesting

To present yourself in the best light, follow these rules no matter what situation you find yourself in:

Arrive early: Plan ahead. Find out what you are and are not allowed to bring into the building. Leave extra time for traffic, parking, security, stopping by the restroom, getting yourself calmed down, and chatting with your attorney.

Turn off your phone: You will irritate the judge beyond measure if your phone rings. Turn it completely off. A vibrating phone can still make noise, and it may tempt you to look at it.

Control your reactions: Your spouse or their attorney may say things about you, your marriage, your children, or your finances that are complete lies, humiliating, or otherwise ridiculous. Often, opposing counsel will do this on purpose to get a reaction out of you. It's a trap, so don't fall for it. Instead, stay in control, keep your face neutral, and remain seated. Don't sigh, scream, roll your eyes, or gesture. Make a note and quietly pass it to your attorney, or discuss it with them during a break.

Answer clearly and briefly: When you are asked to respond, speak clearly and confidently. Maintain eye contact, but don't appear aggressive. Answer questions with a simple "yes" or "no" when appropriate. Try not to answer more than you are asked, and never interrupt. Answer if you're able. If you don't know the answer to a question, then respond with "I don't know" or "I can't recall that." Don't make answers up.

Be honest: There is no faster way to lose credibility with the court than to be caught lying. Hopefully you have been completely honest with your attorney so no surprises come up in court that the two of you haven't discussed and prepared for. No matter how embarrassing it is or damaging you think it might be, if it happens, own up to it.

Don't argue: Do not argue with anyone. Part of being courteous and professional is respecting the process. You will have your chance to tell your side of the story or present evidence. Even if the judge makes a ruling you don't like, stay cool. You may find yourself in front of this judge again, and freaking out may cost you next time.

How to Dress

Dress for court as you would dress for a business meeting. This is no time for jeans, T-shirts, crop tops, or tennis shoes. You may want to make your spouse jealous, but the sexy goddess look isn't appropriate here. Most attorneys recommend conservative, feminine, and off-the-rack. It's going to be hard for the judge to buy your "poor me" argument if you're wearing expensive designer clothes.

Personally, I love it when people express their personality with purple hair, tattoos, and piercings. However, it may cause the court to make assumptions about you that aren't true. Consider removing visible piercings, covering tattoos with clothing, and temporarily returning your hair color to something more natural.

You want to project stable, modest, unassuming, and kind. You are the one that has been trying to do all the right things and follow the rules. A suit, a simple dress, or nice slacks with a blouse and a jacket will be your best bet. Keep accessories to a minimum and your hair neat and simple.

WHAT TO SAY WHEN

If you are particularly outspoken, you may need to learn to speak and behave in a different way to handle divorce proceedings. If your spouse is pulling out all the stops to present you in a bad light, then you will have to counter that by demonstrating that you are the stable, reasonable one, not the high-conflict person.

This shift can be hard for some. They bristle thinking they're giving up their voice, letting their partner get away with things, or not speaking their truth.

Here's the thing: Remaining calm is the only way to be successful against a high-conflict person. The payoff for biting your tongue may mean getting the assets you deserve, or in extreme cases, retaining any custody rights with your children.

It doesn't matter how you feel. Say what the judge or mediator wants to hear, and do things the way they like to see them done. These are important actions to convey:

- I have attempted in good faith to negotiate an equitable agreement.
- I am only interested in what's best for our children.

- It's important to me that our children maintain a good relationship with their mom/dad.
- I have made every effort to communicate in a friendly and factual manner.
- I have complied with requests and followed orders to the best of my ability.
- I am expecting to curtail my lifestyle quite a bit. I am requesting far less than I am used to living on.
- A positive co-parenting relationship is important to me.
- The lack of financial support has put me (and our children) in a very difficult position.
- I have been as flexible as possible in accommodating requests for parenting time changes.
- I have encouraged the children to spend time with their mom/dad.
- I have done my best to keep the details of our divorce private.
- I only speak about their mom/dad in a positive manner.

CHAPTER SIX

PARENTING CHILDREN THROUGH DIVORCE

The most supportive thing you can do for your children to help them cope with and recover from the divorce is to co-parent as successfully as possible. Even if your partner is trying to make things difficult, you have the power to model good behavior. And remember, if you're in a custody battle, both your parenting and interaction with your spouse are being examined under a microscope.

If this is your first time parenting on your own, it's a big adjustment, and you'll need some support and new strategies to make it work for you and your children.

PARENTING SOLO OR APART

Parenting without a partner is a different experience. If you're sharing custody, you have two new opposite realities to get used to—sometimes parenting on your own, and other times not parenting at all.

Like any major life change, there are good and not-so-good parts of solo parenting. Because it's easy to focus on the negative and what's hard, let's first take a look at a few of the awesome parts of solo parenting or parenting apart. Then we'll peek at a few of the challenges and tips for making things easier on yourself.

Solo Parenting Pros

There's less tension.

> Your kids are protected from the day-to-day conflict and tension that used to permeate your home. Distance between you and your partner is also probably giving your nervous system a chance to calm down. Most of my clients reported feeling an immense sense of relief once they were physically separated from their high-conflict partner and said it made them a better parent.

You can parent your way.

> Without your partner around to undermine or criticize your parenting decisions, you can now be the firm, consistent parent your children need without obstruction. They can count on knowing each day what to expect in your home. You can set the rules and expectations that are best for your

kids. You can't control the other parent's home, but you can offer consistency in yours.

Your bedroom is yours.

> It's all yours now. Use the flowery sheets or the ones with penguins. Take down the NASCAR picture, the hunting picture, or that one with the weird colors. Sleep diagonally or invite the animals and kids to join you. Eat pizza and ice cream in bed. Leave crumbs if you want. Don't make the bed if you don't feel like it.

You control the remote.

> No more suffering through those sports, history, cooking, or scary shows (or whatever you hate—no judgment if those are your thing). Delete them from the DVR and record the stuff you want to watch. No more giving up watching your programs. Dog shows? Check. Fashion week? Check. Documentaries? Check.

The menu can evolve.

> Couldn't have salmon because your partner didn't like it? Eat it every day this week. Your spouse wanted a low-carb, super healthy meal every night, but you and the kids get a hankering for fries? Perfect, McDonald's run it is. Or maybe your spouse ate only pizza, burgers, and wings? Now you can crank up the healthy and serve all the veggies you want.

You'll discover alone time.

> If you're sharing custody or the children have visitation time with their other parent, you'll get a few hours or even overnight to recharge your battery. It's nice to use this time to catch up on chores and errands, but don't forget some

"you" time also. Meet up with friends, take in a movie, go for a bike ride or a hike—something you don't get to do when you're on parent duty.

Solo Parenting Cons

Your partner still isn't a good partner.

> Being married was hard, and co-parenting is sometimes even harder. They're late, change schedules, fail to pay their share, and do things just to be mean. It's hard to stay on the high road in front of your kids when someone is being that petty and hateful.

> One client's ex not only returned the children's clothes, including sweaty sports uniforms, dirty and unwashed (which is typical behavior), but one time returned a bag of clothes covered in vomit.

There's nobody to vent to.

> We've all had them—one of those horrible days when you just want to come home and have someone to talk to who will listen and make it better. Solo parenting often means keeping it to yourself or relying on your pet to be your sounding board.

Sick days are on you.

> If you get sick or hurt, you no longer have built-in backup. In the middle of high-conflict divorce, asking your partner to pinch hit for you will either be met with an emphatic "no" or will be used against you as evidence that you aren't keeping your parenting agreement. This is where your BFF Backup and Taskmaster from chapter 1 come to your rescue.

> And when the kids get sick, you'll be the one taking off work if it's your parenting time, unless you have a Plan B in place. If your nine-year-old has a baseball game, but the two-year-old is sick, you'll have to get creative.

Money may be tight.

> I hope you're one of the lucky ones who hasn't been victimized by financial tricks and that your partner is at least supporting you and the children until things get finalized. Or that you earn enough to keep the lights on and groceries in the fridge. But for many, day-to-day life includes wondering how you're going to make it. It's a frightening thing to worry if you have enough food or enough gas to get to work.

Work is work.

> If you've been working, you're already used to the routine of getting kids up and going. If you've gone back to work because money is tight, this may all be new to you: getting up early, putting on something other than comfy clothes, getting the troops out the door and off to school or daycare earlier than usual. Either way, without a partner to back you up, last-minute meetings or schedule changes can throw you a curveball.

Social situations change.

> The third wheel. That's what you might feel like trying to keep up connections with the couples you used to socialize with. It's hard to be a single in a group of couples. And if they were friends of both of yours, you could be faced with probing questions about your divorce. Don't hesitate to fall back on your scripts from **What to Say When** (page 23).

You also might be in the presence of "Switzerland" friends (see page 182) or disloyal "friends," so be cautious what you share.

You'll discover alone time.

> Yes, this can be a pro and a con. I include alone time here, too, since some people find this time to be the hardest. When their children are with the other parent, they may feel lost, alone, and purposeless. When your life has been focused on your children, especially if you're a stay-at-home parent, the hours the children are gone can feel empty and go by slowly if you don't have anything else going on.

Dating is not a good idea yet.

> Because we're in the section called "During Divorce Proceedings," the bad news is that you shouldn't do it. In some states, it's still considered adultery if you aren't legally divorced, and that could have a very negative impact on your case. If you are fighting over custody, your partner will look to show how your new love interest is making you a bad parent. Finally, it's important to recover and heal from the stress and trauma of high-conflict divorce first.

Making It Through

Ask for help.

> There is no shame in asking for help. People in your life want to show up for you, they just don't know how. Whether it's babysitting, cutting the grass, fixing a leaky pipe, bringing dinner, or just providing company, you probably have people who are just waiting for you to ask. Think about

what would be most helpful to you and then reach out. You might be surprised.

Ditch the guilt.

> You're stressed, your world has been turned upside down, and now you're parenting on your own. Perfection is the enemy, and guilt is a wasted emotion—tell them both where to go. For now, focus on loving your children well and spending time with them. All the rest can wait. Resign from obligations such as volunteer stuff you didn't want to do anyway. Say no to ironing or changing towels every day. Eat on paper plates. If you can't afford to eat out, invite your friend over for frozen pizza. No guilt.

Get support.

> I know, I say it every chapter: Having the right support for yourself can make a profound difference. Whether it's a therapist, a divorce coach, and/or a good therapeutic support group, you need some "been there, done that" people in your corner who can validate your feelings and give you tools to keep your head in the game.

Seek financial stability.

> Constantly worrying about money will keep anyone on edge. Take a good look at your budget and determine where you can cut back. Next, determine how you can add to your income. Babysitting, pet sitting, weekend catering jobs—be creative. Watch your budget closely and try not to send out more than you're bringing in. Then begin to think longer-term and make plans to create even more financial stability for you and the children.

MAKING A CO-PARENTING PLAN

Ideally, you will have some temporary orders in place while your divorce is being finalized. If you don't, check in with your attorney and determine when you might have a hearing scheduled for a judgment on temporary orders.

If you are mediating or attempting to negotiate a dissolution with the assistance of your attorney, your interim parenting plan agreement will be less formal than a court order.

Whether you have temporary orders or just a written agreement, I recommend using one of the many co-parenting apps available (see Resources, page 185). Co-parenting with a high-conflict person is exhausting, and just keeping up with the documentation of all their bad behavior will seem like a second job some days. These apps take some of this burden off you and have protections in place to prevent some dirty tricks. You can even request that using one of the co-parenting apps is part of your parenting agreement.

Important Components of the Plan

Your attorney or a quick Internet search should be able to provide you with the parenting plan guidelines for your state or local area. You will need to establish agreement around the following items. Refer back for more information about custody (page 95) and visitation (page 97). It should include:

Child support—Which parent is the payor, the amount, and how it will be paid

Legal custody—Who will be in charge of decision-making for the children

Physical custody—Who is the residential parent

Parenting schedule—Specifically, when the children will be with each parent

Medical, dental, vision insurance, and expenses—Who will cover the children and how non-reimbursed expenses will be shared, reported, and reimbursed

Other expenses—Who will pay what, and how reimbursement or expense sharing will occur. When dealing with a high-conflict person, a verbal agreement is never sufficient. If you have young children, think ahead and include all expenses that you believe might come up for your child, such as:

- Clothing
- Daycare
- School tuition, uniforms, and supplies
- School lunches
- Extracurricular activities, fees, and equipment/supplies
- Auto insurance, fuel, and maintenance
- Haircuts and personal expenses
- Cell phone
- Prom, homecoming, and other special-occasion clothes and expenses
- College entrance exams
- College visits
- College tuition, books, and expenses

It's important to detail not only how the expense is to be shared, but how the parties will notify each other of the expense, how payment will be made, and within what time frame the payment should be made. The more specific, the better. Leaving things too general just opens the door for the high-conflict person to find a loophole and will leave you frustrated.

Without a legal agreement in place, it will be difficult to get a high-conflict person to negotiate or even come to agreement on anything. You will have your work cut out for you attempting to do it on your own. Here are a few tips that will help you stand your ground:

Set a Firm Schedule

We've talked about the importance of making sure that you are seen as promoting a relationship between the children and their other parent. Suggest a schedule that you believe is reasonable, and then stick to it.

If you or your spouse work unusual schedules (police, firefighter, shift work), then suggest a time split based on number of hours per month and schedule that month (or every two weeks) as soon as the work schedule comes out for the next period. If that person fails to communicate their work schedule within X days so that a parenting schedule can be coordinated, then they will forfeit their parenting time for that period.

Be specific. That is critical with high-conflict people. Allow no wiggle room because they will just keep pushing.

Communicate in Writing

If you aren't able to use a co-parenting app, e-mail is your next best option. Phone calls with a high-conflict person can easily get out of hand and you'll have no documentation as to your agreement. You want to be able to show written proof that your partner agreed to the visitation schedule or the expense sharing that they are now not complying with.

See Sharing Information (page 126) for ideas to communicate about the children.

Document

Document the efforts you have made to come to an agreement and to follow the temporary court orders. Also, document any behavior by your spouse that is uncooperative or not in the best interest of the children. Make notes if your partner picked the children up or dropped them off late, if they took them out of state without approval, or failed to pay expenses. Write down any nasty comments your partner makes in front of the children, or anything your children relay that they experienced at their other parent's house.

You Can Say No

You don't have to agree to schedule changes or other variations to an agreed-upon parenting plan. Yes, you want to demonstrate that you are cooperating, but continued requests for changes, particularly last-minute ones, do not need to be agreed to. You won't decrease their anger or high-conflict behavior by being accommodating. You'll simply set a precedent that they can continue to do whatever they please without regard to the agreement.

Don't Take the Bait

Your spouse will try everything to get you to react, back down, or give up. You deserve a fair settlement and your children deserve to have you in their lives. Keep your cool, speak assertively, and respond as discussed in chapter 1 (page 7). The way to win with a high-conflict person is to manage your emotions and not give them any fuel for their arguments.

Kids First

Every action and decision in divorce should be made with the best interest of the children in mind. That includes your language, behavior, parenting, and cooperation with your co-parent. Unless proven otherwise, the court will work under the assumption that civil co-parenting and "equal-ish" time with each parent is best for the child. They assume that because it's usually true.

Regardless of how your spouse is behaving, it's still critically important to take the high road—both for your children and to advocate for yourself in divorce.

SHARING INFORMATION

As a general rule, you should share anything that you would want or expect to be notified about. Withholding things from your partner won't help you look cooperative to a judge when it comes to making your custody argument. Again, it doesn't matter how you feel; it matters that the mediator, magistrate, or judge believes you are committed to successfully co-parenting. So, smile and share.

Neglecting to communicate with the other parent can also have negative and unexpected consequences. For example, what if you both take your child to the doctor for a cold and are both giving them antibiotics? Or the new medicine interacts with another medicine that the other parent didn't know they were taking? What if you both take your children for dental checkups? Getting their teeth cleaned twice can't hurt, but do you want extra X-rays taken?

Information to be shared might include:

- School schedules and calendars
- Teacher, IEP, ISP, or other meetings
- Sports and activities schedules
- Social activities (birthday parties, family weddings, play dates)
- Religious activities
- Work schedules for teens
- Medical treatment (completed or scheduled)
- Behavior problems
- Homework projects or upcoming exams
- Grades
- Friendship or relationship issues
- Any adjustment or mental health concerns

A co-parenting app with a scheduler and message function makes this easy to do; however, there are other ways to accomplish it as well:

- Add the co-parent to any school, sports, or activities e-mail notification list. That way, they will get their own copy and you won't be responsible for remembering to share.
- Ask teachers, coaches, doctors, and so on to communicate with both of you regarding your child. Then you're both receiving the same information and the burden is not on you.
- If the co-parenting relationship is stable enough, pass a notebook back and forth when the children switch homes.

Each parent dates a new entry and provides an update for the other parent. Copies of schedules and such can be passed with the notebook. There are some obvious disadvantages to this method: It's not time-sensitive, records can be destroyed or lost, children might have access (sensitive information should not be shared in this way).

* An online alternative to the notebook would be an online instrument that you can both edit and add your entries to. Schedules or other important documents can be scanned and added as well.

Note: A caution about shared calendars: Horror stories abound of parents sharing an online calendar. One parent goes in and makes a change without notifying the other parent. Then when that parent is not home for the drop-off or doesn't show up for the dance recital, it is used against them in a custody action as evidence of poor co-parenting or lack of dedication to the children.

HOW TO RESOLVE COMMON ISSUES IN CO-PARENTING

Co-parenting with a high-conflict person is bound to be filled with struggles. My advice to you is this: Your high-conflict partner is not going to follow the rules of decency when it comes to co-parenting. Decide right now that you will stop fighting to change things you cannot change.

You have the ability to either take the conflict up a notch or dial it back. Escalating the conflict isn't good for you or your kids. I'm not suggesting that you become a doormat. What

I am saying is that if your spouse always sends the clothes back dirty even though you asked them to send them back clean, let it go. Choose your battles. Only fight the ones that really matter.

So, what are the issues that matter and how can you attempt to resolve them?

Schedule Changes

You want to be flexible with them so they will be flexible with you. What if you get the chance to go on a great boating trip and want to swap weekends? Shouldn't you extend the same courtesy? Ideally, yes.

So, assume best intentions and accommodate their request. Then ask them for a parenting time change and see how they respond. If you're not getting what you're giving, then the schedule stays the schedule. Period. It's harder on you with no flexibility, but it's one less battle you have to fight with them.

Expenses

If you've gotten temporary orders or made an agreement, the types of expenses and how they will be paid should be clear. Otherwise, best practice would be to scan the receipt and attach it to an e-mail explaining what the expense is, what the other parent's share is, and when/how you are requesting payment. Typically, 14 to 30 days is reasonable for reimbursement. If you don't receive payment by the date requested, send a brief e-mail reminder asking for payment. If they owe you for more than one outstanding receipt, continue to send monthly statements listing each individual item and the total amount owed.

If you have court orders outlining your partner's responsibility, you may be able to show them to a school, doctor, or sports team so you are only financially responsible for your share. Some will honor this arrangement and hold the other parent accountable for the remainder of the balance.

It is, unfortunately, common for high-conflict people to be financially abusive. They don't care that it hurts their children. If the behavior continues and what they owe becomes excessive, you may need to ask the court for relief.

Information Sharing

The other parent should be sharing information with you just as you are sharing with them. If that isn't happening, arrange to get yourself added to the school or activity e-mail or notification system. Call and explain your situation.

Involving the Children

You know it's best not to bad-mouth your spouse or put the children in the middle, but that may not stop your partner from doing it. They may tell the children things that are untrue, use the children as spies or messengers, or say things about you in front of them.

In chapter 3, under Ways Children React (page 54), I introduced the idea of giving your children agency, or a voice. When you model healthy behavior, foster openness and authenticity, and teach your children age-appropriate information, you're guiding them to be able to make their own assessments of what is true.

Keep doing what you're doing. Your partner may think they're winning, but they will lose in the long run. They'll lose the respect of their children who will eventually see through the manipulation and will use their voices to speak up against it.

Nine years after her divorce, Kristina says her 19-year-old finally understood. He said:

"I get it now—it's a Dad problem, not a you problem."

EXCEPTIONS TO CO-PARENTING

If your partner has been abusive, has an addiction or mental illness, or otherwise puts the children's safety at risk, act surely and quickly. Talk to your attorney and find out what steps you need to take. Request sole custody and a protection order. Ask for supervised visitation only. Request these at least on a temporary basis until the court has a chance to investigate. Have your documentation ready and be prepared to prove your case. "He said/she said" may not be enough to win the day.

Ask that a guardian ad litem be appointed. This is an attorney who will act as a neutral third party on behalf of your child and may testify as an expert witness.

Note: Without the backing of the court, it's dangerous to prevent your spouse from seeing the children even if you have concerns. The court may view this as uncooperative or adversarial on your part.

WHAT TO SAY WHEN

Co-parenting with a high-conflict person can range from mildly frustrating to rage-inducing.

Your spouse knows how to push your buttons because they installed them. Having some scripts or responses ready to go can help you maintain your emotional boundaries:

- That doesn't work for me.
- I'm afraid I can't accommodate that.
- I will consider that and get back to you.
- Our agreement is that you will pick the children up at 5:00 p.m., not 6:00. Please be on time next week.
- Please communicate any requests for scheduling changes directly with me and not through the children.
- I have already provided that schedule to you twice. If you need another copy, feel free to contact the school directly.

- The tuition for school is due next Friday. I have paid my portion and let them know you are responsible for the remaining balance of X.
- [Child] has a doctor appointment on [date] at [time]. Are you able to take them or would you like me to do it? Please let me know by [date].
- [Child] has been invited to a birthday party a week from Saturday from noon to 3:00 p.m. at [place]. Since that is during your parenting time, I wanted to check with you before responding. I will have [child] call you tonight to discuss it.
- I bought [child] new soccer cleats last week and spent X. [Other child] needs a new swimsuit and googles, so please take them shopping this weekend to get them. The expense should be approximately the same, but let me know if there is a difference and we can split it.

PART
THREE

AFTER THE DIVORCE

Finally. The papers are signed, and you're officially divorced. It may not have been easy, but now you can take a deep breath and think about what's next.

However, "what's next" can be tricky when you've been through high-conflict divorce. Your ex may not be satisfied to let things go. I hope that you are allowed to move on in peace, but I want you to be prepared in case you have some post-divorce fallout.

The effects of high-conflict divorce can linger long after the ink dries on your agreement, so chapter 7 will introduce a few of the psychological concerns you may have. Chapter 8 addresses the subject of post-divorce considerations, like your ex failing to make payments or taking you back to court. Finally, chapter 9 will offer some tips for co-parenting and caring for your children after divorce.

CHAPTER SEVEN

MOVING ON

It's okay to grieve. The Holmes-Rahe stress scale rates divorce as one of life's most stressful life events, second only to death of a spouse or close loved one.

That's because divorce itself is a tremendous loss. Many people experience a deep sadness that their marriage has ended. Even if you're partying in the streets that it's over, don't be surprised if you get hit by some feelings later on.

WHAT GRIEF CAN LOOK LIKE

Let's examine what the stages of grief might look like for you during and after divorce:

Denial: A failure to acknowledge the reality or pain of divorce may cause feelings of numbness or make you want to isolate. Denial is our way of not facing the pain of all that we've lost.

Anger: Getting angry can feel good. This isn't what you planned, things are hard, and/or you've been treated unfairly. You're mad. And you deserve to be. Just make sure you get your anger out in a safe and healthy way.

Bargaining: In this stage, you can get caught up in second-guessing and beating yourself up with guilt, thinking what if you'd acted this way or that way. By spending time thinking you could have changed the past, you're still not feeling the full impact of your loss.

Depression: This is where true mourning happens. I prefer to call it sadness or the dark night of the soul. All the emotions you've been putting off are finally demanding to be acknowledged. You may cry at unexpected times, reminisce about all the old times or the future you won't have, be more sensitive, or move in slow motion. Let the feelings come; honor them now so you can let them go.

Acceptance: You're going to be okay. Maybe not today, but you can see a future for yourself where you aren't sad or angry. You begin to take steps to put the pieces of your new life in place and have a sense of hope. You're developing a new identity and are ready to explore new pathways.

Not everyone will experience all five stages, nor do they go through them in order. Grief is very personal. Each one of us moves through these stages at our own pace. Be gentle with yourself.

If you find yourself stuck in any one of these stages for a long period of time, or feel like it's holding you back from moving on with your new life, please reach out for support. High-conflict divorce is a big bump in the road, but it shouldn't be a complete road block.

THE RIGHT KIND OF RUMINATION

Chapter 4 explained that rumination can be one of the emotional impacts of high-conflict divorce. But the right kind of rumination can also help you move on after divorce. Deliberate rumination can help us process and grow from the traumatic experience.

We talk to ourselves all the time. Whether you realize it or not, you're doing it right now. The way we talk to ourselves affects us in the present moment, and it can also change our long-term thoughts and behavior. Put simply, the quality of our thoughts creates our experience of life.

Deliberate rumination involves actively taking hold of those repetitive negative thoughts and purposefully examining them. It's an opportunity to create a new narrative and rebuild what the trauma has shattered. When an intrusive thought comes up, try one of these strategies:

Journal your thoughts. Experts believe that simply writing about the event and your emotions can help you integrate the experience into your life, rather than let it define you.

Reflect on your strengths. Talk to yourself like you would a good friend. What strengths did you show during the traumatic time, or what growth have you noticed in yourself since the experience?

Get into problem-solving mode. Brainstorm potential solutions to the problems you are ruminating about.

Distract yourself. Go for a walk, call a friend, meditate, or go to a movie. Do something that will temporarily interrupt the cycle. You'll be able to deal with concerns in a more deliberate manner after you've regained a sense of control.

Although trauma may leave us with scars, it doesn't prevent us from being transformed.

LONG-TERM IMPACTS OF STRESS

In chapter 4, we discussed the difference between normal stress and chronic stress. Depending on your experience, you may be feeling stress that just doesn't want to go away.

Chronic stress can cause:

- Elevated blood pressure and risk for stroke or heart attack
- Increased risk for type 2 diabetes
- Digestive trouble, including heartburn, nausea, constipation, and diarrhea
- Tight muscles, causing headaches, back and shoulder pain, and body aches
- Irregular, heavier, and more painful periods; increased symptoms of menopause
- Weakened immune system

WAYS TO MITIGATE STRESS

Life will never be completely stress-free, but here are some steps you can take to reduce the impact of chronic stress:

Make lifestyle changes.

> Start with the basics. Are you getting enough sleep, eating right, and getting some exercise? Give your body and brain the foundation they need to rebuild from stress. Consider some of the options in chapter 4 that can help you calm your nervous system, such as meditation, a yoga class, or a daily reading or journaling practice.

Identify the source.

> Have you ever just felt "off"? Irritated, forgetful, tired, sore, sweaty, lonely, sad, or overwhelmed, and you're not quite sure why? That's a cue to stop and consider the source.

> What's changed recently? Any new stresses or unresolved issues? Are you ruminating? Are you experiencing new emotions? Are you afraid of something? If you can identify the source of your feelings and symptoms, you can find the right tool to help address it.

Change it or let go.

> Once you identify the source of your current stress, ask yourself if this is something within your control. If it is, create a plan to make changes. Otherwise, look for ways to release your grip so you can focus your time and energy on positive things, like making the best of your new life. If it's out of your hands, put it out of your mind.

TRUSTING OTHERS AGAIN

Nothing beats you up like being betrayed, lied to, or victimized. The person you trusted to be your life partner turned into an enemy. Maybe the family court system didn't provide the justice you expected, or people you thought were friends failed to have your back.

After a high-conflict divorce, it's normal to have trouble with trust. You may even have trouble trusting yourself. After all, you didn't see the red flags last time—how do you know you'll recognize them now?

Life is not meant to be lived in isolation. We are wired for connection and intimacy. And deep intimacy with friends and loved ones requires trust. You may be wary right now, but you can learn to trust again. Try to:

Take your time. Learning to trust again is a process, not an event.

Review the past. Look back and see if you failed to trust yourself.

Question the source. Consider where this distrust is coming from.

Get support. Share your feelings with a coach, therapist, or support group.

Start small. Don't share too much too early in a new relationship.

Pay attention. Listen to your own intuition and inner wisdom.

Listen to your body. Learn when your body is telling you something isn't right.

Watch your comfort zone. Be wary of someone who tries to push your boundaries.

Assume best intentions. But speak up and clarify if something feels hurtful.

Look at behavior. Has this person kept their promises?

Expect mutuality. Is this person trusting you, too?

Learning to trust again can be a "two steps forward and one step back" process. Be compassionate with yourself as you continue to develop your sense of trust again.

IDENTIFYING WHAT YOU WANT

What do you want? It seems like such a simple question. But if you've been in a difficult marriage or dragged through a high-conflict divorce, you probably haven't been contemplating your life or your dreams—you've been in survival mode.

Debbie described her reawakening this way:

"You don't realize how broken your marriage is until you get out of it. You will start to see the crazy that you thought was normal, in your ex and yourself. Your ex will try to define you to you and your kids and to others in the warped, ugly way that they have, but you have to redefine yourself and stop believing the lies he/she says about who you are."

Now that it's over, you can take a breath and think about you again—about the kind of life and future you want for yourself. It's true that life may not have turned out the way you thought it would, but what if I told you it could be even better? Brighter, more peaceful, more fulfilling, and more life-giving? It's time to dream again.

Where to Start

If you've put your own dreams on hold for so long that they seem unrecognizable now, it's time to get out your trusty journal or laptop and ask yourself some questions.

For yourself:

- What energizes me?
- What drains me?
- What am I passionate about?
- What kind of home environment do I want?
- What does my ideal day look like?
- What would financial security look like for me?
- What kind of friends do I want to have around me?
- What kind of work would support me financially? Emotionally? Spiritually?
- What healing do I still need to do?
- Where do I want to live?
- Who was I before marriage and children?
- What do I think I'll do for fun?
- Where would I like to travel?

If you have children:

- What kind of home do I want them to live in?
- What kind of parent do I want to be?
- What kinds of values do I want to teach?
- What behaviors do I want to model?
- What kind of adults do I want to surround my children with?

Is anything beginning to come into focus? Let's look at some general categories.

Categorizing Goals

Finances: What does your post-divorce budget look like? Are you comfortable? Does it support your financial goals? If not, what steps do you need to take to align your financial life with your other dreams?

Home: Do you live in a home or city you love? What short-term changes can you make in your home to make it more enjoyable? Would you like to live somewhere else? Buy a new home? Move to an apartment? A different city? What would it look like, and what would it take to make it happen?

Work: Are you doing work that makes you feel good, either because you're helping others or because you're supporting yourself? Is there something you'd rather be doing? Are you reentering the workforce after being home for years? What kind of work appeals to you, and what would you need to do to work in that field?

MAKING A PLAN AND SETTING GOALS

Hopefully you've identified some things you want in your new life. Now it's time to make a plan to turn those dreams into reality.

It can be overwhelming to look at that big goal and think about all the work required to make it happen. But if we break that big goal down into small steps, it feels more manageable. An ancient Chinese proverb says:

"It is better to take many small steps in the right direction than to make a great leap forward only to stumble backward."

Building the Framework

If you've thought it through and are ready to make a big change in your life, here's how to get started:

1. Identify specifically what you want to accomplish and when.
2. Brainstorm the steps/tasks that need to be done.
3. Choose where to start.
4. Monitor and adjust as necessary.

Most people find step two to be the most difficult, so give yourself plenty of time. The most important thing is to get started.

And remember, a plan can be changed, so don't worry about it being perfect. Make a first draft of your action plan and start by choosing just one thing, a baby step, and do it. Make a phone call. Look something up on the Internet. Visit a gym. Gather up your bills. Any small action will let you start checking things off and feel that sense of accomplishment that you're moving forward.

Let's look at an example. Cindy wanted to work as a hairstylist by the time her children were in sixth grade. That meant she had two years to accomplish her goal. Her first draft looked something like this:

1. Research and choose a school.
2. Apply for aid and save money.
3. Secure childcare and rides for kids.
4. Get licensed and apply for jobs.

As she researched schools and learned more, she was able to add more specific tasks to each category and assign target dates to each.

Whether you're reentering the job market, exercising to get in the best shape of your life, or working to create financial security; breaking that big, faraway dream into small steps will help you keep moving forward and improve your chances of success.

WHAT TO SAY WHEN

When you've been through a high-conflict divorce and the related trauma, it's common to occasionally get caught up in negative thinking. The best way to combat those negative thoughts is to replace them with a truth or more positive statement. Think about what you would say to a friend.

Negative Thought: There's no way it will ever work.
Positive Statement: This seems difficult, but I've come up with creative solutions before.

Negative Thought: I'll never be able to get a job.
Positive Statement: This is a challenge, but I can tackle it. I can keep trying new things and looking for more help.

Negative Thought: This is the worst thing that's ever happened.
Positive Statement: This has been really hard, but look how much I've grown.

Negative Thought: People keep hurting me on purpose.
Positive Statement: There are some people who don't deserve my energy. Instead, I will focus on the people who love me and show up for me.

Negative Thought: I'll never trust anyone again.
Positive Statement: What I've gone through is making it hard for me to trust people, but I will keep working on it. I know there are trustworthy people in the world.

Negative Thought: I'm going to be angry for the rest of my life.
Positive Statement: I am working on letting go so I can focus on my future instead of my past.

CHAPTER EIGHT

SECURING YOUR FUTURE

In a standard divorce, there is a period of discord or conflict, and then an agreement is signed and both parties go on to live their own lives. In high-conflict divorce, just because the battle is over doesn't mean the war is won.

That ex who stirred up conflict and drama during the divorce might be determined to continue their antics post-divorce. Or perhaps you have some major cleanup to do after the dirty divorce tricks they played. This chapter will cover some common scenarios and offer suggestions for handling them.

WHAT IF I HAVE TO GO BACK TO COURT?

There are many valid and legal reasons that one of you may take the other back to court for post-decree modifications or orders. And then there are nuisance, dramatic, and downright vengeful reasons your ex may try to pull you back in.

Support Modifications

In chapter 5, we discussed that child support is always modifiable and spousal support typically is. Either of you may choose to return to court to ask for support to be increased or decreased based on a change in circumstances. The most common reasons would be a change in income, cohabitation by the payee, or a change in custody.

Custody Modifications

Parents might find that the original custody arrangement is not working. One parent may be requesting additional time with the children or documenting that the other parent is not sharing the parenting as originally agreed. If child support has been calculated based on 50/50 shared parenting and that gets changed to 70/30, then support will be adjusted accordingly.

In extreme high-conflict cases, signs of parental alienation or neglect may be seen. If you suspect this, and/or your ex is returning to court to fight for additional visitation or full custody, consider enlisting the services of a parenting coordinator or guardian ad litem.

Relocation

If either parent is planning to move, and relocation makes a prior parenting plan impossible to maintain, the parties may need to return to court (or mediation) to establish a new parenting plan. As always, the best interests of the child will be considered in any decision.

Child Abuse/Neglect Allegations

Your ex may still attempt to paint you as an irresponsible or abusive parent to give them an additional "win" and reduce their child support payments. Ideally, you have been using a co-parenting app, putting your children first, and taking good care of yourself.

No Contact/Restraining Order Request

Your ex may allege that you have been harassing or being abusive toward them. If you have been regulating your emotions and following the recommended response method (page 7), it is unlikely that this request will gain any traction.

WHAT IF MY EX STOPS PAYING SUPPORT?

What if you have a high-conflict ex who doesn't care that there's a court order requiring them to pay child support or spousal support and they simply stop paying? This can be a nightmare if you rely on that money to pay your living expenses.

Double check your decree. Make sure you understand exactly what was ordered and when and how it was to be paid.

Find out the reason. Send your ex a written message asking (and documenting) why support payments have stopped. They may have gotten sick or lost their job, or maybe they're just being mean. Either way you'll know.

Consider alternatives. If you ex responds and they are having trouble making the full payment, ask if they can at least make a partial payment for now and catch up later. Some is better than none.

Make an emergency plan. You're already living on less and now your ex is making it impossible. The only option is to find a way to deal for now. Can you pick up extra hours at work? Cut back on expenses? Ask the bank to let you skip a payment or pay interest only on a loan? Even if you take your ex back to court, it can take weeks or months for the court to take action. In the meantime, you and the kids need to eat.

Work through your state agency. Contact your local support enforcement agency to inform them of the situation and find out what steps you need to take.

Take legal action. Notify your attorney to determine your rights, and find out if it's appropriate to file a violation order with the court.

Do not restrict visitation. Even if your ex isn't paying child support as ordered, withholding visitation is against the rules. Child support and visitation are separate issues, and you could face trouble by refusing your ex access to the children.

WHAT IF YOUR PARTNER RUINED YOUR CREDIT?

Financial sabotage is common in high-conflict divorce. If your ex negatively impacted your credit score, there are a few steps you can take to get things back on track:

Pay on time. This is rule number one for rebuilding your credit. Lenders want to see that your recent history shows no late payments and that you're making progress paying balances down.

Reduce interest rates or payments. If you're having trouble making payments on time, call your creditors and ask them to reduce your interest rate or minimum payment. Most creditors would rather you keep up with some payment than fall behind.

Review your credit report. Check your report on all three credit bureaus (TransUnion, Equifax, and Experian) and note any derogatory remarks or late payments that are incorrect or that you may be able to explain.

Dispute negative items. Credit bureaus are obligated to investigate once you lodge a dispute. When you dispute, provide a detailed explanation as to why you believe that item should not appear on your report.

Save your history. Don't close all old accounts. Part of your credit rating is based on having longer-term credit accounts. If you have accounts in your name only that have a zero balance, consider leaving them open for now.

Avoid new accounts. Each new credit inquiry puts a little dent in your credit rating, so don't apply for any new credit accounts (not even to save 15 percent on that big store purchase) until your score is built back up.

Start with a secured card. If you have no credit, consider getting a secured card. You put $500 in the bank as a guarantee, and they give you a card with a $500 limit. You charge on that card and pay it off each month to create a credit record.

Become an authorized user. If you have a family member with a great credit rating who you trust to pay on time and who trusts you, ask to be added to their account as an authorized user. Their payment history will also be reported under your name and help you establish a good credit history.

WHAT IF THEY STOPPED PAYING BILLS?

I advise my clients to establish terms in their agreement that will not rely on the ex to make payments on anything that would affect them. If your ex has failed to make your rent, mortgage, utility, or car payments, you can face a whole host of problems. Your power could be shut off, your car repossessed, or you could be evicted. Not to mention the possible damage to your credit rating if your name is associated with any of the accounts. If your ex stops paying:

Check your decree. Make sure you understand exactly what payments were ordered and when and how they were to be paid.

Communicate directly. Ask your ex in writing why they aren't making the payments as agreed.

Pay the bill. If your ex won't pay, it's up to you to keep the lights on, your car in the driveway, or the landlord off your back while you await relief from the court.

Make an emergency plan. Find ways to stretch your budget to cover the extra expenses until you can get court relief.

Take legal action. Notify your attorney to determine your rights, and find out if it's appropriate to file a violation order with the court.

HOW DO I GET THE RETIREMENT BENEFITS I'M DUE?

A written or oral agreement is not enough to ensure that you get your share of your ex's retirement account or pension benefits. Even if it is written in your divorce decree, there are steps you must take to protect yourself financially.

Division of retirement benefits is a complicated topic. Different accounts require different documents, and different employers have different rules. There are also tax consequences to consider.

In general, most retirement and pension plans (other than IRAs) require a QDRO (qualified domestic relations order) in order for the plan administrator to divide the asset. Each account requires a separate QDRO, which should be prepared by an attorney as part of your divorce process since they must be signed by both you and your spouse.

Follow up to make certain that any QDROs have been accepted by the plan trustee or administrator and properly executed. In some cases, your share of the account must stay with your ex's employer, but will be set aside in an account under your name. Other times, you can withdraw the money and set up your own account at the place of your choosing.

You must roll any distributions directly over to another retirement account in order to avoid paying taxes. In addition, you have a one-time opportunity at divorce to avoid paying the 10 percent early withdrawal tax penalty if you are under $59\frac{1}{2}$. You will still pay income tax on any money not reinvested in a retirement account, but you won't pay a penalty.

WHAT TO SAY WHEN

Requests for post-decree modifications can look very similar to the divorce process, including hearings, discovery, and so on. Your course of action will vary depending on the level of conflict and complication.

  If you receive notice of a post-decree action, do the following:

Contact your attorney. Call or e-mail them to discuss your strategy and best options.

Pay attention to dates and deadlines. Review the notice or letter carefully for instructions, court dates, deadlines, or other action items.

Provide any information requested. Gather, copy, and provide any documents requested in the notice.

Attempt to settle out of court. The courts always prefer that parties come to their own resolution, so do your best to negotiate an agreement via mediation or attorneys.

Do not retaliate. Do not limit visitation, withhold support payments, harass, threaten, or otherwise act out against your ex for bringing the action against you, no matter how ridiculous.

Comply with current court orders. Review your decree to ensure that you are following all provisions.

Build your defense. Document your income and expenses, review notes about your parenting or your ex's parenting, children's adjustment or behavior, or whatever you need to counter the claim.

CHAPTER NINE

CHILDREN'S NEEDS AFTER DIVORCE

Children need time to adjust to divorce. Switching back and forth, seeing each parent less, having different rules at each home, and other changes can be difficult for them. Likewise, co-parenting may not be easy, and protecting children from that requires diligence. This chapter will provide examples of common co-parenting issues, offer ideas for addressing them, and help you set your children up for success.

MAINTAINING THE CO-PARENTING PLAN WITH A HIGH-CONFLICT EX

Once the divorce is finalized, you should have a parenting plan and written agreement that specifies custody, visitation, and other details of how you and your ex will work together to co-parent your child(ren).

In a standard divorce, both parents follow these agreements or communicate and work with each other to negotiate changes as needed. They both put the child first and have a high level of trust in each other. Co-parenting with a high-conflict ex may, unfortunately, not go as smoothly. As always, your best approach is to choose your battles, know exactly what your agreement says, and continue to document any violations. Here are some common occurrences and suggestions for handling them:

Late Drop-Offs/Pick-Ups

Be prepared for your ex to show up late for visitation with the child(ren) or drop them off later than the agreed-upon time. This is the ultimate power play and gives them the feeling that they are in control.

First, try using the response method discussed in chapter 1 (page 7) to send your ex an e-mail reminding them of the parenting agreement guidelines. Something as simple as, "Our parenting agreement says that you are to pick up [or drop off] the children by [time] on [day] for your parenting time. Because you've have been more than [X] minutes late the last two weeks, I wonder if you would like to discuss an alternative schedule? Otherwise, I would appreciate it if you would be on time or discuss changes with me in advance."

Continue to document all occurrences.

Schedule Change Problems

Schedule changes can be a one-sided relationship with the high-conflict ex. They will expect you to get on board with any last-minute requests or parenting time swaps they request, but will be unwilling to accommodate any modifications you ask for.

Try to address the issue directly with them. "I have tried to be accommodating and have agreed to your parenting time change requests on [list dates]. However, you have denied the changes I asked for on [list dates]. I am asking you to grant me the same courtesy by being more flexible in the future."

If they are being particularly demanding or unreasonable, you have the right to say "no" and default to your written visitation agreement. Continue to document all occurrences.

Delay in Paying Expenses

Most parenting agreements include some provision for splitting children's expenses. First, refer back to your decree to double-check that it is an agreed-upon expense and you have submitted it in accordance with your agreement.

Keep track of each expense, what it was for, the amount the other parent is responsible for, how you notified them, and the date you notified them. E-mail monthly statements to your ex with a reminder note. Keep your comments simple, such as, "I have included a statement of the outstanding expenses that you are due to reimburse me for. Some of these are past due, so please let me know when I can expect payment."

Disneyland Parent Syndrome

Some high-conflict co-parents like to pretend that parenting is a competition and they want to win the "best-liked parent" award. They may not enforce the same rules regarding meals, bedtime, or screen time that you do at your house. In addition, if your ex has the means, they may buy the children clothes and electronics or take them on vacations that you can't afford to match.

It's best to just let it go. You can make a friendly request to your ex to curtail the luxury gifts, but be prepared for it to fall on deaf ears. The kindest thing you can do for your child is be as excited as they are, without bad-mouthing their other parent or complaining about your own lack of money. I know this is easier said than done. But it's not your child's fault. Keep loving them and let them enjoy their gifts, with the mind-set that the gifts of love and stability that you give them are so much more valuable.

OPTIONS IF YOU CAN'T AGREE

If you aren't able to communicate and negotiate directly with your ex about these issues, then you'll need to decide if this is a battle worth fighting. Start by asking yourself, what's best for the children?

Following a high-conflict divorce, it's not uncommon for co-parenting problems to arise. Sometimes the best option is not to co-parent, but to parallel parent. You aren't able to work as a team, so you do your part, they do their part, and you learn to let go of any expectation that you have control over how they parent.

If you have joint custody or a shared parenting agreement, then each of you will make decisions for the children when they are in your care (unless your parenting plan says otherwise). If your ex is not sharing information with you, be certain to double-check with doctors, dentists, pharmacists, and others before giving your children medication or treatments to ensure you aren't duplicating.

If your ex refuses to respond, negotiate, or comply with any of your requests, then you have three options:

1. **Live with it.** Consider their schedule request changes as they work for you, deal with the drop-off/pick-up issues, pay the expenses yourself, and ignore the Disneyland act. This is you choosing not to fight this battle in order to reduce the level of conflict.

    If you choose this option, make it a conscious choice. Get support to help you decide if this is right for you and process any negative feelings. Then find peace in it; let go of any resentment and don't retaliate.

2. **Bring in a parenting coordinator or mediator.** This person will help you work through parts of the parenting plan that aren't working or that the two of you can't resolve. A professional, neutral third party can often create a bridge for negotiation.

    Sometimes parenting plans need to be revised and you need expert help to sort it out. Search for someone who has experience with high-conflict people, and they may be able to help you facilitate a new agreement.

3. **Take it to court.** If the issue becomes enough of a burden, it may be necessary to return to court to order a change or enforce a prior agreement. You don't want to be running off to court every time they are 30 minutes late or owe you 100 dollars. On the other hand, there are times when the children are not getting what they need, or their noncompliance is impacting your work or financial situation.

Don't make empty threats about taking your ex back to court. Continue to try to communicate via e-mail or your co-parenting app and negotiate on your own. Document occurrences and violations. If you decide that legal intervention is necessary, don't threaten—just do it.

Always consider what is in the best interest of the children. If the children will be negatively impacted if a change isn't made, then living with it may not be an option. Take your time to make the right decision. Get good counsel from a coach, therapist, or attorney.

WHEN CHILDREN NEED EXTRA ATTENTION

Results of a 10-year study clearly indicated that a successfully reestablished family or a successful remarriage can improve the quality of life for both parents and children. After high-conflict divorce, the struggle is getting to your own version of a "successfully reestablished" family. If the level of conflict continues, or your ex uses the children as pawns or messengers, arriving at this goal can be delayed, and your children may require some extra help to get acclimated to the new family structure.

Most children bounce back from the initial upset of divorce after a period of adjustment. Going back and forth between houses, keeping track of schedules and belongings, or remembering which parent to check with can feel burdensome at first. Experts say it takes about a year for children to recover from the impact of divorce. Every child is different; every family is, too. But if things are handled right, over time the children can end up healthier than if the parents had been unhappy but stayed together.

In the meantime, feelings of anger, sadness, resentment, and confusion are all normal. Refer back to chapter 3 (page 54) to review some typical reactions children have to divorce.

Signs to Watch For

Your child should continue to improve and adjust as time passes, but be on the lookout for some indicators that they aren't adjusting well:

School: If you notice a consistent trend of uncharacteristically poor performance or disinterest, reach out to the teacher and guidance counselor. It can really help explain the situation—a teacher will be more sympathetic if they understand what's going on, and the guidance counselor can offer support and a safe outlet for your child to express themselves.

Friends: Social connection is one of the ways we heal—kids included. If your child is isolating from or breaking off friendships, it may be time to get them some extra support.

Parent Problems: If a child refuses to visit one parent, villainizes one parent, or aligns too strongly with one parent, it's a good idea to get to the bottom of what's going on.

Immediate Dangers: Some signs of adjustment problems that require immediate, professional intervention would be:

- Physical violence
- Suicide threats
- Property destruction
- Self-harming behaviors

Your child's life and safety are at stake. Don't hesitate to call 911 or local law enforcement for help in an emergency.

Ali was aware of the high level of conflict and had been observing her children for any signs of trouble.

"My son seemed to be doing fine. He wasn't having trouble in school or with friends. He hadn't expressed any concerns to me. But I noticed that I kept finding lots of hair in his room and in the bathroom. One night I leaned in close and saw that he had pulled quite a bit of his hair out. That's when I knew he needed more help."

As a parent, you know your children best, so stay observant and be a good listener.

Helping Your Children

As parents, we never want to see our children in pain. It goes against everything in us. Focus on these four principles to offer your children the best foundation for recovery:

1. **Do your own work to regulate your emotions.** If you are not regulating your own negative feelings about the divorce, your children will pick up on that. Children and teens shouldn't feel responsible to help regulate their parents' emotions.

2. **Maintain open communication.** When you are calm and can handle discussions, your children will be more likely to come to you with questions and concerns. You'll shut them down if you fly off the handle or cry every time they mention the other parent's name.

3. **Watch for signs, but allow space.** Be observant, but don't crowd them either. We all need space when trying to process difficult emotions. Just keep maintaining that open and loving environment so they feel free to come talk to you when they're ready.

4. **Teach them the beauty of resilience.** Take this opportunity to teach them by example that when life throws us a curveball or someone hurts us, we can choose to overcome it without bitterness or resentment.

Providing Extra Support

You can find support for your children in family, friends, church, a school psychologist, a child counselor, or a school support group. Many clients have told me that their children found it helpful to be with other children whose parents divorced. There are at least three good reasons to get extra support for your children during and after divorce:

1. **It takes a village.** From an African proverb, this means that children grow up safe and healthy by being looked after by a whole group of people. You can't be everything all the time. Your children benefit from having a safety net of others around them who are also committed to their welfare. Let others help with meals or rides to practice. Swap babysitting with a friend. Create your own community of family that depends on each other.

2. **They listen to others.** Have you ever noticed that you can say something to your child and it goes unheard, but if someone else says the same thing, it's like new information to them? That's reason number two for having extra support for your children. It doesn't matter who they hear these important messages from, as long as they hear them. If Aunt Becca or their youth leader can get through to them, awesome!

3. **Different can be good.** Everyone has their own outlook on the world and their own lens of experience. Provide your children with other adults who can offer a different view than you; others who can hold space and listen to them without judgment.

While you're at it, be aware of the opinions of anyone who may spend time with your children. Debbie's 10-year old son returned home from private Catholic school one day and said:

"The priest told me that you and Dad are going to hell if you get remarried. Is that true?"

Be vigilant about making sure that the people you and your children depend on are safe to talk to, so they don't end up causing more hurt.

Life isn't perfect and neither are we. Making it through divorce and co-parenting with a high-conflict ex will take tremendous self-restraint and every parenting skill you have. When we do what's best for our kids, we make the world a better place. And they're worth it!

WHAT TO SAY WHEN

When you keep the lines of communication open, you'll know what your kids are thinking and be able to address their questions. But some of those questions may be really hard to answer! Here are some common scenarios and possible answers:

Dad/Mom got me a great big TV for my birthday. Why don't I have a TV in my room at your house?
That's awesome—what a great gift. But you know that your mom/dad and I make different choices and things aren't the same at each house. At this house, the rule is no TVs in the kids' bedrooms. But aren't you lucky to get to have one at your mom's/dad's?

I never have to do chores at Dad's/Mom's house. Why do I have to do them here?
That's great, really. It gives you more time to spend with your mom/dad. But in this house, we are a team. I believe that all people who live in a home should be responsible for helping to take care of it. And I really appreciate how you've been pitching in.

Why do I have to share a room with my stepsister/brother at Mom/Dad's house? I hate them.

That sounds really difficult for you. It must be hard to share your space with someone you don't get along with. Would you like to talk about some ways you can talk to your mom/dad about how you're feeling?

Mom/Dad said I could come live with them all the time if I wanted to. Can I do that?

Right now, your mom/dad and I have agreed that this parenting plan works best for everyone involved. Is there something that isn't working for you? We want to have a plan that works for all of us.

QUICK GUIDE TO COMMON SITUATIONS

Although every divorce is unique, high-conflict divorce does have some scenarios that come up again and again. Your ex may be angry, hostile, trying to ruin your reputation, or worse. As tempting as it may be to lash out in retaliation or try to vigorously defend yourself, I hope I have effectively conveyed how remaining calm and polite is in your best interest.

When you allow your emotions to take over, you aren't able to make good decisions, be the best parent, protect yourself, or make a favorable impression on the court. All of these affect your ability to have a good outcome. And a calmer you is a healthier you—don't let that person raise your blood pressure anymore!

Here are some guidelines for coping with common situations that you may come up against:

GENERAL RULES

When dealing with a high-conflict person in any situation, there are a few rules you can follow to save your sanity:

Limit contact. Minimize the amount of contact you have, in person and in writing.

Don't expect them to change. If they've been difficult, expect that behavior to continue.

Get it in writing. Make sure every detail you can think of is included in your divorce or separation agreement.

Only respond if necessary. Not every question or statement deserves a reply.

Don't rely on them. Take care of things yourself whenever possible.

Take the high road. Don't retaliate or stoop to their level—simply document their antics.

Vent to safe people. Share your feelings with a trusted person so they don't stay bottled up.

Be made of Teflon. Try not to let anything they say or do stick to you.

HOSTILE E-MAILS OR TEXTS

If you have children, I highly recommend that you do all your communication through one of the many co-parenting apps available. If that isn't possible or you don't have children, then do any communicating in writing and follow these tips:

Determine if a response is even necessary. Many hostile messages sent by your ex don't require a reply. They are simply monologues about what a terrible person you are, and what they're going to do to take you down. Simply screenshot the e-mail/text and print it out in the event that you need it later on.

Respond in writing. E-mail gives you more opportunity to consider your words and provides a good evidence trail. Keep it short, simple, polite, and straightforward.

HOSTILE PHONE CALLS

Taking phone calls from a high-conflict person can be like walking into a field of landmines. In a phone conversation, you have no control over what you hear, you may be recorded, and you have no record of what was said to you. You may also be more likely to say something that isn't in your best interest or that you will regret. If your children are within earshot, they will hear the conversation, see you rattled and be subjected to the conflict. Instead:

Conduct all communication in writing. Don't answer the phone if they call you. If you see a call from your ex, send them an e-mail asking them what they need. In extreme circumstances, you may even need to block their number.

Keep calls between parent and children. You may have provisions in your parenting plan that call for your ex to have phone calls with the children on certain days or times. If your children don't have their own phones, then the other parent will be calling on your phone. Hand the child the phone and let them pick up, or answer and ask them to hold while you pass the phone to your child—no conversation is necessary.

FAILURE TO RESPOND

The opposite of those hostile calls, texts, and e-mails is silence. And this can be even more frustrating. You can ignore a nasty e-mail, but if you need to get some important information and your partner or ex won't reply (or has blocked you), you're stuck. Suggestions:

Review your divorce decree. Follow the decree or any written agreement you have.

Do your own thing and don't worry about them. You inquired, and they didn't respond. If your ex's parenting time is supposed to start at 5:00 p.m. on Friday, and your decree says that they forfeit their time if they're more than 30 minutes late, then you can take the children and leave at 5:35. Document the time and your actions and carry on. You don't need to get in touch with them at all.

Do your part to investigate. If you are trying to find out about insurance coverage, call the insurance company or your ex's employer yourself. If they aren't paying bills, paying support, or following through on court orders, ask your attorney about options.

Frustrating you is part of their plan. The silent treatment is a form of abuse and control. Try not to let it ruin your day, because it's not something you can change. Remind yourself that's why you aren't with this person anymore.

DEROGATORY/INFLAMMATORY SOCIAL MEDIA POSTS

In this day of social media, it's common for high-conflict partners or ex-spouses to rant to friends, family, and anyone who will listen. These folks love nothing more than to get attention, play the victim, and spread rumors. You can:

Close down shop for now. Shut down or lock down all your social media accounts during divorce. You don't want your partner or anyone else to have access to your accounts or see what you are posting. Similar logic applies after divorce.

Watch your own step. Be very cautious about what you post and who can see it. Social media could be used as evidence for custody or support modifications.

Unfriend and block. If you must stay on social media, block them and anyone who supports them, including their family members. The less you see, the better. You know the truth and the people who care about you know the truth. That's all that matters. Anyone who believes lies about you isn't on your team.

CORRESPONDENCE TO FRIENDS/ FAMILY

High-conflict people love to plead their case to others. They may even reach out to your camp, describing all the terrible things you did to them, how you were unfaithful, how you abused them or the children, how you hid or stole money, or otherwise wronged them. Here is my simple advice:

> Do nothing. The best way to find out who these people truly are is to do nothing. Don't reply to or defend yourself against your ex's garbage. Think about it. What would you do if you got an e-mail from your friend's spouse or your sister's ex with all kinds of outrageous claims? If you're a person of character who truly knows and cares for your friend or your sister, you wouldn't believe it, and you would reach out to them to show your support.

In my experience, one of three things happen when you don't respond:

1. You never hear from that person; therefore, you can assume that they believe the lies. Do nothing and delete them from your circle.
2. They contact you but have an accusatory tone or line of questioning. Ask them straight out: *What percentage of that story do you believe is true?* Then act accordingly. If they automatically assume that you cheated on your spouse without any evidence or confirmation, they are not for you.

3. They contact you and are shocked that your spouse or ex is saying these things. They assure you they know none of it is true, and they hand you the correspondence to keep and use as evidence if necessary. These are your keepers.

Be wary of Switzerland friends or family members. I've said this before, but when your ex is spreading vicious rumors and trying to ruin you, it is not possible for a person or couple to remain "friends" with both of you. Either they are 100 percent for you or they aren't. Anyone who can remain friends with a person who behaves like your ex is behaving is not someone you want around.

CALLS/E-MAILS TO YOUR WORKPLACE

High-conflict individuals may stretch beyond and harass you at work or contact your employer. They may want to rattle you or could be trying to get you fired. In this case:

Be upfront. Have a conversation with your manager to let them know what is happening and get their input on the best way to proceed. You don't need to be specific; simply say, "I have gone through/am going through a very difficult divorce and my ex has begun to harass me here at work. I just wanted you to know this. If you have any advice to protect myself and my position, I welcome it."

Go next level if needed. If your manager isn't helpful or doesn't have the authority to assist you, contact your human resources department for direction. If you work for a smaller company that doesn't have such procedures in place, contact your local law enforcement for help.

CONTACTING YOUR CHILD'S SCHOOL

It's all about exerting control and authority for a high-conflict personality, so your spouse or ex may approach your child(ren)'s school to make sure they know who the "good" parent is. In this case:

Keep school in the loop. Be certain the school is aware of any custody or no-contact orders and has copies on file. Discuss any concerns with the principal, guidance counselor, or teachers. School officials don't need to know everything, but they should be told that you're going through a contentious divorce and be made aware of any safety issues. They can also help you be on the lookout for any reactions or changes in behavior your child may be exhibiting.

FLAUNTING THE NEW LOVE INTEREST

Because your ex is driven by a need to hurt you, they may take every opportunity to put their affair partner or new love interest in front of you. It's their hope that this will embarrass you, make you feel bad, or wish you were still with them.

They may post all over social media, or show up at every one of your child's events displaying way too much public affection with their new friend. They may even purposefully show up at the same places they know you frequent.

Ignore them. Do your absolute best to simply ignore them. Bring your own friend or family member with you to create a barrier and give you strength.

Work to heal and count your blessings. Do your own inner work so you can get to the place where it honestly doesn't bother you. Come to the peaceful conclusion that this high-conflict person is someone else's problem now. Please do not let their bad behavior deter you from living your best life.

RESOURCES

HOTLINES

National Domestic Violence Hotline: 1-800-799-SAFE (7233)

National Suicide Prevention Lifeline: 1-800-273-TALK (8255)

BOOKS

Baker, Amy J.L., and Paul R. Fine, LCSW. *Co-parenting with a Toxic Ex: What to Do When Your Ex-Spouse Tries to Turn the Kids Against You.* Oakland, California: New Harbinger Publications, May 1, 2014.

Bishop, Gary John. *Unf*ck Yourself: Get Out of Your Head and Into Your Life.* New York: HarperOne, August 1, 2017.

Eddy, Bill. *BIFF: Quick Responses to High-Conflict People, Their Personal Attacks, Hostile Emails and Social Media Meltdowns.* Scottsdale, Arizona: Unhooked Books, September 16, 2014.

Landers, Jeffrey A. *Divorce: Think Financially, Not Emotionally: Volumes I and II.* San Clemente, California: Sourced Media Books, January 8, 2015.

Smith, Kristi. *DREAM...A Guide to Grieving Gracefully: 5 Keys to Unlock the Grip of Grief.* Abundant Press, November 17, 2015.

WEBSITES

Woman's Divorce: www.womansdivorce.com
Divorce Magazine: www.divorcemag.com
Headspace: www.headspace.com
The High Conflict Institute: www.highconflictinstitute.com

PODCASTS

Breaking Free: A Modern Divorce Podcast, with Rebecca Zung, Esq., and Susan Guthrie, Esq.
Divorce and Your Money, with Shawn Leamon, MBA, CDFA.

CO-PARENTING APPS

Our Family Wizard: www.ourfamilywizard.com
Co-Parently: www.coparently.com

SUPPORT GROUPS

DivorceCare: www.divorcecare.org
Alcoholics Anonymous: aa.org
Narcotics Anonymous: na.org

REFERENCES

Allen, Summer, Ph.D. "The Science of Gratitude." A white paper prepared for the John Templeton Foundation by the Greater Good Science Center at UC Berkeley. Last modified May 2018. ggsc.berkeley.edu/images/uploads/GGSC-JTF_White_Paper-Gratitude-FINAL.pdf.

American Institute of Stress. "Stress Effects: How Is Stress Affecting You?" Last accessed June 18, 2019. www.stress.org /stress-effects#effects.

Banschick, Mark, MD. "The Ex Who Wants to Hurt You." *Huffington Post.* Last modified December 30, 2011. www.huffpost .com/entry/the-ex-who-wants-to-hurt_n_1171962.

Bishop, Gary John. *Unf*ck Yourself: Get Out of Your Head and Into Your Life.* New York: HarperOne, August 1, 2017.

Callahan, Tracy. MA, CDC®, Florida Supreme Court Certified Mediator, in discussion with the author, May 24, 2019.

Centers for Disease Control and Prevention. "Physical Activities Guidelines for Americans: 2nd Edition." Accessed June 5, 2019. www.health.gov/paguidelines/second-edition/pdf /Physical_Activity_Guidelines_2nd_edition.pdf#page=55.

Dictionary.com. "Trauma." Accessed June 2, 2019. www.dictionary.com/browse/trauma.

EMDR Institute, Inc. "What Is EMDR?" Accessed June 4, 2019.www.emdr.com/what-is-emdr/.

Gingell, Sarah, PhD. "How Your Mental Health
Reaps the Benefits of Exercise." *Psychology Today.*
Last modified March 22, 2018. www.psychologytoday
.com/us/blog/what-works-and-why/201803
/how-your-mental-health-reaps-the-benefits-exercise.

Haden, Jeff. "12 Simple Steps to Repair Your Credit and
Increase Your Credit Score." *Inc.* Accessed June 21, 2019.
www.inc.com/jeff-haden/12-simple-steps-to-repair-your
-credit-and-increase.html.

Hawley, Katherine, PhD. "Trauma, Trust, and Time: When
Trauma Undermines Trust, It's Hard to See a Brighter
Future." *Psychology Today.* Last modified September 3, 2017.
www.psychologytoday.com/us/blog/trust/201709
/trauma-trust-and-time.

Headspace. "How to Meditate." Accessed June 15, 2019.
www.headspace.com/meditation/how-to-meditate.

Kingan, Cassie, MA, LPC, CCPC, CCTP, Trauma Specialist, in
discussion with the author, May 29, 2019.

Law, Bridget Murray. "Probing the Depression-Rumination
Cycle: Why Chewing on Problems Just Makes Them Harder
to Swallow." *American Psychology Association Monitor on
Psychology.* 36, no. 10 (November 2005): 38. www.apa.org
/monitor/nov05/cycle.

Matthew, Daniel. "30 Percent of Divorces Involve Face-
book: What You Need to Know."DivorceMagazine.com.
Last modified June, 5, 2018. www.divorcemag.com/
articles/30-percent-of-divorces-involve-facebook/.

Mayo Clinic. "Positive Thinking: Stop Negative Self-Talk to Reduce Stress." Accessed June 21, 2019. https://www.mayoclinic.org/healthy-lifestyle/stress-management/in-depth/positive-thinking/art-20043950.

National Conference of State Legislators. "Child Support Guideline Models by State." Last modified February 20, 2019. www.ncsl.org/research/human-services/guideline-models-by-state.aspx.

Ohio Department of Child and Family Services. "Basic Child Support Schedule." Accessed June 10, 2019. www.odjfs.state.oh.us/forms/num/JFS07767/pdf/.

Selhub, Eva, MD. "Nutritional Psychiatry: Your Brain on Food." *Harvard Health*. Last modified April 5, 2018. www.health.harvard.edu/blog/nutritional-psychiatry-your-brain-on-food-201511168626.

Smith, Kristi. Author of *DREAM . . . A Guide to Grieving Gracefully*, in discussion with the author, May 20, 2019.

Sowald, Heather G. "Divorce Courts Divide Assets and Liabilities Equitably." Ohio State Bar Association. Last modified May 26, 2016. www.ohiobar.org/public-resources/commonly-asked-law-questions-results/divorce-courts-divide-assets-and-liabilities-equitably/.

Tartakivsky, Margarita, M.S. "How Trauma Can Trigger Positive Transformation." *PsychCentral*. Last modified July 8, 2018. www.psychcentral.com/blog/how-trauma-can-trigger-positive-transformation/.

The Tapping Solution. "What is Tapping and How Can I Start Using It?" Accessed June 4, 2019. www.thetappingsolution .com/what-is-eft-tapping/.

Wisconsin Department of Children and Families. "Child Support Percentage Conversion Table." Accessed June 10, 2019. https://docs.legis.wisconsin.gov/code/admin_code/ dcf/101_199/150_a.pdf.

INDEX

ACKNOWLEDGMENTS

Working with betrayed, confused, angry, hurt, and traumatized people is not a career that many would choose on purpose. Yet, I feel immensely satisfied knowing that my clients are more confident and better protected, make smarter decisions, and recover more quickly as a result of having the right professional support. My hope is that this book helps many others achieve those same outcomes.

There are so many people who have poured into my life and into this book that I cannot possibly thank or acknowledge them all. My children have been my biggest supporters and encouragers, calling, texting, and bringing Starbucks at just the right time. I pray every day that I am becoming the parent they deserve. Since losing both of my parents, my brother and only sibling has been my rock. I can simply never repay him or show enough gratitude for all he has done to help me get to the point in my life where I can share a book with the world.

Many professionals I am blessed to call friends spent hours sharing anecdotes and giving me access to their incredible brains to provide the best possible legal, psychological, and parenting information for you. Florida Supreme Court–certified mediator Tracy Callahan, MA, CDC®, took time away from her busy practice to share her knowledge of mediation and co-parenting. Trauma specialist Cassie Kingan, MA, LPC, CCPC, CCTP, generously offered her experience with personality disorders and clinical psychology. Michelle Maciorowski, attorney at law, always made time to have lunch or take phone calls to provide her legal expertise. Certified divorce lending professional Shannon Ryan took me out for margaritas when things got hard and shared many financial insights.

Kristi Smith, author of *DREAM . . . A Guide to Grieving Gracefully,* gave me a deeper understanding of grief, prayed over me, brought me unhealthy food, and believed in me before I believed in myself. And finally, special thanks to my roommate Tammy Pratt, who respected my space when the office door was closed (a lot), prayed for me, and did my share of chores for longer than anyone should have to.

There is a special group of women—you know who you are—who have been my sisters since the day we met and have supported and encouraged me like only sisters can. We've shared so much heartbreak and so many tears, but have also found laughter and joy amid the ashes. We found each other in tragedy and stay together in triumph.

And because our own life experiences shape much of who we are, I'd like to thank my first ex-husband for always being there, putting our kids first, and making co-parenting work the way it should. And my second for teaching me the hard lessons I now use to serve my clients so well.

Of course, none of this would have been possible without the trust and honesty of my clients. They've taught me so much about life, hurt, pain, grief, recovery, and resilience, and my life is richer for it.

Finally, I thank God for never leaving my side and for allowing me the privilege to protect those who need it most.

ABOUT THE AUTHOR

Debra Doak specializes in helping women make hard decisions about marriage, money, and life. She is a CDC Certified Divorce Coach® and Certified Divorce Financial Analyst® who is committed to giving women the confidence they need to speak up for what they deserve, in their marriages or at the negotiating table. Debra believes that knowledge is the antidote to fear and that planning well for divorce creates better outcomes for everyone. She can usually be found petting a cat and has two adult children who are changing the world. You can find her at DebraDoak.com or on Instagram @debradoakcoach.